Raising Boy Readers

Raising Boy Readers

MICHAEL SULLIVAN

an imprint of the American Library Association

HURON STREET PRESS

CHICAGO • 2014

MICHAEL SULLIVAN began his career as a special needs teacher, then spent fifteen years as a children's librarian and library director in public libraries. For five years he taught library science at Simmons College in Boston. He has been a chess teacher, a coach, a storyteller, and a juggler, as well as a program supervisor at the Boston Museum of Science. He has written several books for librarians and teachers, including *Connecting Boys with Books: What Libraries Can Do*, *Connecting Boys with Books 2: Closing the Reading Gap*, *Serving Boys through Readers Advisory*, and *The Fundamentals of Children's Service*, all for the American Library Association. His books for children include *Escapade Johnson and Mayhem at Mount Moosilauke* (Big Guy Books, 2006), *Escapade Johnson and the Coffee Shop of the Living Dead* (PublishingWorks, 2008), *Escapade Johnson and the Witches of Belknap County* (PublishingWorks, 2008), *Escapade Johnson and the Phantom of the Science Fair* (PublishingWorks, 2009), and *The Sapphire Knight* (PublishingWorks, 2009).

© 2014 by the American Library Association

Published by Huron Street Press, an imprint of ALA Publishing
Printed in the United States of America
18 17 16 15 14   5 4 3 2

Extensive effort has gone into ensuring the reliability of the information in this book; however, the publisher makes no warranty, express or implied, with respect to the material contained herein.

ISBNs: 978-1-937589-43-1 (paper).

Library of Congress Cataloging-in-Publication Data

Sullivan, Michael, 1967 August 30–Raising boy readers / Michael Sullivan.
    pages   cm
  Includes bibliographical references and index.
  ISBN 978-1-937589-43-1
  1. Boys—Books and reading—United States. 2. Teenage boys—Books and reading—United States. 3. Reading—Sex differences—United States. 4. Children's literature, American—Bibliography 5. Young adult literature, American—Bibliography. I. Title.
  Z1039.B67S855 2014
  028.5'5—dc23

                                                            2013011537

Cover design by Casey Bayer. Image © Juriah Mosin/Shutterstock, Inc.
Text design by Kim Thornton in Dispatch and Mercury Text.

♾ This paper meets the requirements of ANSI/NISO Z39.48-1992 (Permanence of Paper).

*This book is dedicated to Cathie Sue Andersen,
who not only put up with me during the writing
of it, but helped me work through more questions
about children's books than anyone can imagine.*

Contents

Introduction

So you have a son or some other boy in your life? You want him to grow up to be a reader? Maybe you worry that if he doesn't read well, he won't succeed in school, or in life. Maybe you worry that if he doesn't read well, he won't go to, or finish, college. Maybe you worry that he will grow up lacking empathy or social skills. Maybe you just hate the idea that he will live a life without the constant joy of reading. Well, congratulations: all of these are great reasons to want to raise a boy reader.

And all of them seem to come out of fears that are very common these days. Boys don't read well—at least, not as well as girls. Boys don't read enough—at least, not as much as girls. Boys don't read good books, or books at all. And because boys don't read, they are putting their futures in danger.

In some ways, all these fears are well grounded. In many ways, they are just like any other fears: they feed on themselves and grow until they blot out reason and clear thinking. In all ways, giving into these fears only makes things worse.

This book comes out of my experience of twenty years as a special needs teacher, a public librarian, a youth sports coach, a chess teacher, and a researcher and writer on the topic of boys and reading. I have long written for and trained the professionals—teachers and librarians—on how to turn boys, often reluctant or resistant readers, into avid, lifelong readers. At the same time I have spoken to many parent groups about how all this research and methodology affects them, day to day, trying to raise boy readers. I am thrilled to finally be able to address this last and most important audience directly in this book.

This is what the experts know. This is what the research says. And hopefully, this is presented in a way that is practical and useful. Know that for all that we teachers and librarians try to do, parents and families have so much more effect on developing readers. Indeed, I tell the professionals all the time that if they really want to change lives, then their job is not to serve children but to support parents, who ultimately spend more time with their kids and have a greater influence. If you are reading this book hoping to better guide a boy toward being a lifelong reader, then you are the key to solving the boy reading problem, and I salute you.

There are a few ideas that run throughout this book, and it is worth getting them on the table right up front. These points will come up over and over again, in many forms and in many settings, but they should not be lost in the details. Keep them in mind as you travel through the book.

Speaking in General Terms

When we talk about boys and reading, we are necessarily talking about big generalities. Every child is an individual, and nothing we say can apply to all kids, or all boys. This can be a real problem when it paralyzes us. Every child is unique, so how can we do anything but look at one child and try to figure out what is going on in his head?

While acknowledging that all children are individuals, there are general trends that we can look at that will help us understand what we are seeing when we consider an individual child. When it comes to gender and reading, I like to talk about what I call the GI Joe–Barbie spectrum. Think about a broad range of behaviors and characteristics from the most prototypically boy traits on one side (the GI Joe end of the spectrum), to the most prototypically girl traits on the other side (the Barbie end of the spectrum).

Now most children will not be found anywhere near the edges. Kids just aren't that easy to pigeonhole. In fact, you will find boys showing reading characteristics even over on the half of the spectrum that we would consider to be more associated with girls, and that is fine. What is important is that a lot of boys will fall in a big bell curve right in the middle of the boy half of the spectrum. That is why we consider these behaviors to be generally boylike.

Knowing what is common among boys when it comes to reading means we can better understand why many boys read the way they do, and use some common strategies to help them become better, more independent readers. That is important because so many boys have reading problems. Being a typical boy reader means you read a year and a half below girls of the same age, on average, throughout your school years.[1] By the time you reach the eleventh grade you are reading three years below the average girl.[2] Being an average boy reader means you read only 2.3 hours per week.[3] Being an average boy reader means you have a better than 30 percent chance of being in remedial reading by the time you are in the third grade.[4] If we can identify ways many boys read, we can look at ways to alleviate many of these reading problems.

Now here is the big warning. Just because many boys *do* read a certain way doesn't mean that this is how they *should* read. If you have a boy who reads confidently, independently, who drives his own reading and chooses books that are far from the types I talk about as "boy reading" in this book, well, leave him alone. He is doing just fine. Nothing says that there is a right way for boys to read—only a common one. Indeed, boys that differ greatly in their reading from what I describe are less likely to have reading problems in the first place. But if you do see a boy who is reluctant to read, who talks about reading being forced on him, who rejects all the books that adults want him to read, and who steadfastly identifies himself as a nonreader, then you have a boy that is probably approaching reading in many ways common to his gender. There will be a great deal in this book to help you. And, by the way, if you have a girl who reads, or refuses to read, this way, everything here applies to her as well.

Stress

When I first started thinking seriously about boys and reading, people wanted a silver bullet, some trick or technique that would unlock the hidden reader in boys. I was constantly asked if phonics or whole language was the right approach, if one canned reading program or another "worked" (however you define that), or if a certain teaching style made for better readers. I looked at all these, at hundreds of teaching methods and approaches, at any number of "programs" for home or school use. (I will address many of those questions in the pages that follow as well.) Some had more promise than others, some could be discounted as useless, but none really addressed the most important issue.

In more than twenty years in the business of reading, I have come to believe that the biggest issue keeping boys from becoming readers is stress. Everyone recognizes the bad numbers; everyone knows that on average boys do not read as much or as well as girls. Boys pick up on that fact early. When a boy does fall behind in reading, well-meaning parents, teachers, and librarians leap to intervene. Often it is a high-stakes standardized test that identifies a boy as having a reading deficiency. When a significant number of his peers start suffering reading problems, he identifies with those who look like him. There is so much stress around boys and reading, that many boys decide reading isn't for them long before it can become a lifelong habit. That is why the boys' reading problem is not so much a matter of skill or illiteracy as one of motivation, what we call *aliteracy*—having the ability to read and no compulsion to do so.

The National Assessment for Educational Progress (NAEP) reported that the number of students in general reporting that they read for pleasure outside of school declined steadily from 1979 to 2001.[5] Teachers in the 1970s talked about the rise of reluctant or resistant readers in the seventh and eighth grades; now they are appearing in droves in fourth grade.[6] I am quite sure that these two facts are connected, and they are especially ominous for boys. Boys on average read less for pleasure than girls do and are more likely to be reluctant or resistant readers, so when these trends get worse, then boys are more likely to suffer disproportionately.

This book will look at very real issues that boys face and that make it hard for them to develop as readers, but never forget that artificial, outside stresses beyond the control of the individual boys make all these issues so much worse. The best thing any parent can do to help a boy become a reader is relax.

Choice

Here is a word you will see over and over in this book: *choice* (thirty times at last count; *stress* shows up forty-one times). Ultimately, boys need to have—and feel confident that they have—control over their own reading. This is often the difference between learning how to read and becoming a reader. We will look at any number of ways that parents can give control back to boys, but always remember the simple conclusion that researcher William Brozo reached. Boys who read well almost universally feel like they have control over their reading, and those who don't read well often speak about reading being foisted upon them.[7]

Does that mean taking yourself as a parent or a friend out of your boy's reading life and leaving him to fend for himself? Certainly not. Boys need encouragement, support, and role modeling in their reading, even more than girls do. Isolation in reading is a trait common to boys, one that hurts them as readers. But the goal is not to make your boy read; it is to make him a reader. Unless he takes charge of his own reading, he will likely read only what others make him read.

Facing the Challenge of Boys' Reading

Make no mistake, boys' reading issues are real, and the problems boys have with reading affect their schoolwork, their emotional development, and eventually the options they have for what they want to do with their lives. This means that as a parent or a concerned person in a boy's life, you are bound to have many pressing questions. Questions about why so many boys read, or don't read, in certain ways, and more important, what you can do about it. When I speak to parent groups, I usually start by saying that if anyone has questions, ask them now, because I would rather spend my time answering the questions that you have than standing up like some professor and lecturing for an hour, leaving five minutes for questions at the end. Most nights, I spend the entire time answering questions.

I can't do that in a book, so I will do the next best thing. This book is divided into five chapters addressing the basic questions we all should ask about reading: when, why, how, what, and who? Within these chapters I address the most common questions I get about boys and reading from parents. At the end of each chapter I step aside and look at the bigger, broader questions related to, but somehow beyond boys and reading. Should boys and girls be taught separately? Should boys read girl books? Is whole language or phonics instruction best in school? Are electronic books (e-books) the answer? And are boys' reading problems a product of nature or nurture?

I will also tell some of my favorite stories from more than two decades on the front lines of the boys-and-reading battle. I hope some will make you laugh, some will scare the daylights out of you, and some will just make you mad. Because this is what you want for your boy, that he finds reading so engaging that it becomes real to him. That is what will ultimately keep him reading.

So . . . read on.

NOTES

1. Christina Hoff Sommers, *The War against Boys* (Simon and Schuster, 2000), 14; Donna Lester Taylor, "'Not Just Boring Stories': Reconsidering the Gender Gap for Boys," *Journal of Adolescent and Adult Literacy,* December 2004/January 2005, 292.

2. Lanning Taliaferro, "Education Gender Gap Leaving Boys Behind," *Journal News,* June 17, 2001, 17.

3. Adi Bloom, "Girls Go for Little Women but Boys Prefer Lara," *Times Educational Supplement,* March 15, 2002, 18; Steven J. Ingles et al., *A Profile of the American Sophomore in 2002: Initial Results from the Base Year of the Education Longitudinal Study of 2002* (National Center for Education Statistics, 2005), 75.

4. Carla Hannaford, *Smart Moves: Why Learning Is Not All in Your Head* (Great Ocean Publishers, 1995), 94.

5. Teri S. Lesesne, *Naked Reading: Uncovering What Tweens Need to Become Lifelong Readers* (Stenhouse, 2006), 2.

6. Ibid., 50.

7. Taylor, "'Not Just Boring Stories,'" 294.

When Boys Read

Big Question: Phonics or Whole Language?

When we talk about stressing over boys and reading, the question "When?" seems to be front and center. When should a boy learn to read? Is my boy late coming to reading? What grade level is he reading at? (That is, when will he be reading at fourth-grade level, like he should?) The standardized test says he should be reading at a certain level, but he is only reading at this level—should I be worried? But the biggest question often comes down to why boys so often learn to read, and progress in reading, slower than girls.

It is taken as a given these days that, on average, boys do not read as well as girls. This view is backed up by any number of horrifying statistics. In U.S. Department of Education reading tests, girls scored higher than boys in reading in every year in every age category for thirty years.[1] In 2006 in Maryland, 72 percent of eighth-grade girls read at a proficient level or higher, but only 61 percent of boys.[2] In a 1998 Canadian study of 13-year-olds, 55 percent of girls read at the advanced level, to only 33 percent of boys.[3] The reading gap among twelfth graders is twice as large in favor of girls as the math gap is in favor of boys.[4]

The Brain Lag

One of the natural factors that puts boys behind girls in reading is known as the *brain lag*. Girls' brains simply mature earlier than boys' brains. Girls hit their period of rapid growth and brain development before boys, and remain ahead through most of the school years. At age 2, a girl's vocabulary is 40 percent higher than a boy's.[5] By age 3, girls are a year ahead of boys in language skills. Girls' brains reach their full, adult size at age 11½, on average. Now there is still a good deal of development and gelling to go, but at that point a girl has as much physical brain mass as she ever will. Boys won't reach that stage until three years later, at age 14½.[6]

And here is the good news to lower the stress on parents who have been told their boy is behind in reading: the reading gap between boys and girls can be explained entirely by the brain lag. Boys read a year and a half behind girls, on average, throughout their school years. That gap starts small and balloons to a three-year difference by the time kids are in the eleventh grade. The brain development lag starts as early as age 2, and reaches its peak of three years difference by the time boys are 15 years old. It isn't that boys don't read as well as girls; they simply read at a different time, based on when their brains have developed to a certain point.

Through most of their school days, girls have bigger and better developed language areas in the brain. As girls' brains finish growing and boys' brains start to catch up, the reading gap will disappear as well. Unfortunately, this happens toward the end of high school. Even worse, we do not recognize this difference in brain development. We hold all fifth graders to a single standard of where they should be in reading, when there are a thousand reasons why one fifth grader is at a different developmental level from another. The most powerful of these reasons is gender.

And Should You Care about Reading Levels?

Let us dispense with the idea of "grade-level" reading right up front. You may have heard that your son is reading two years below (or above) grade level, but what does that actually mean? Grade-level reading is a sort of average, the average level at which we expect, say, fifth graders to read. What do you know about averages? Half the kids will be above, and half the kids will be below. If the *average* boy reads a year and a half behind the average girl, than the average fifth-grade boy will be reading nine to twelve months below grade level. Conversely, the average fifth-grade girl will be reading nine to twelve months above grade level.

These are the average kids, not the girls who will eventually be valedictorian or the boys that you would consider to be in academic trouble. What is more, these differences have nothing to do with intelligence or work ethic, but simply the different time schedules their brain development is on. Grade-level reading is a pointless and arbitrary standard. Kids will learn to read when their brains are ready for it, and expecting all kids to meet some benchmark only adds stress to kids and parents. Still, schools will push students to meet these standards that are now being enforced nationally, but as parents you need to know how useless and ultimately damaging they are.

Increased reliance on benchmarks in the age of No Child Left Behind only highlights differences in student achievement (very narrowly defined) when schools should be focusing on instilling the ability to learn in new ways and to think critically. And those differences are stark when it comes to gender. Sixty percent of As in American schools go to girls. Seventy percent of Ds and Fs go to boys, meaning boys fail at twice the rate of girls.[7] Boys are 50 percent more likely to be held back in elementary school.[8] Eighth-grade boys are 50 percent more likely to be held back than eighth-grade girls.[9]

> Major sex differences in function seem to lie in patterns of ability rather than in overall level of intelligence.
> —Doreen Kimura, in *Scientific American*[10]

These terrible statistics are so broad and so consistent that they force us to consider one of a very few explanations. The more cynical approach says that either boys are just naturally less intelligent than girls, or the vast majority or boys are simply lazy, and have been for a long time. Those stands are hard to defend, given the success of boys and men later in life. The more reasonable answer is that boys tend to develop at a different pace than girls, and our attempts to deny that are unfair and unproductive.

Acknowledging the Brain Lag

So how do we address the brain lag? The easiest approach would be to start every boy in kindergarten a year later than every girl. Sure, some boys are ready for kindergarten at age 5, and some girls aren't. But given the overwhelming difference in brain development, starting boys later would at least give kindergarten teachers a better chance of teaching a majority of their students at about the same developmental level. And the need for this kind of approach is increasing every year. Kindergarten today is the first grade of thirty years ago, largely due to increased pressure on early literacy. This trend seems counterproductive: if boys aren't ready to read at age 6, why would we try to make them read at age 5?

> Starting kids reading before they're ready can actually boomerang and turn them off to reading.
>
> —Leonard Sax, *Why Gender Matters*[11]

Let me warn you, that idea can be very unpopular. Any hint of discrimination based on gender is likely to evoke a heated reaction. Still, some parents do try to hold their boys out of kindergarten an extra year, a practice known as "academic redshirting."[12] If you suspect your son might be a bit slower to pick up reading skills, I would encourage you to pursue this route. There is some evidence to support you. Finland consistently ranks first in international reading tests, spends significantly less than the United States on education, and doesn't start formal schooling until age 7. Why? Teach at the appropriate level and boys won't learn to hate school.[13]

The Tipping Point

While kindergarten is often the beginning of boys' reading problems, all the research tells us that the real problems kick into high gear just about the beginning of third grade. That means if you have a boy who is 7 years old who is already reading above the level expected of him, you need to consider these facts:

In 2004, 9-year-old boys scored five points below girls on the National Reading Test, 13-year-old boys scored ten points below, and 17-year-old boys scored fourteen points below.[14] Writing scores were worse. Fourth-grade boys scored seven points below the girls, eighth-grade boys scored eleven points below, and twelfth-grade boys scored twenty-four points below.[15] That is a very steep rise in achievement gaps between boys and girls from third grade on.

In Natrona County, Wyoming, third-grade boys scored 16 percent lower than girls in the state reading test, Proficiency Assessment for Wyoming Students, which is bad enough, but seventh-grade boys scored 45 percent lower than girls.[16] In Alaska, "reading scores begin dropping precipitously for boys in the 3rd, and especially the 4th grades," according to the preliminary research of a Guys Read Pilot Program.[17] This is just a sampling; you can find more examples, probably a few close to your own home.

And just to add to the stress on parents of 8-year-old boys, a Stanford University study linked flagging reading skills with discipline problems. When did these problems start appearing? Third grade, of course.[18]

> If you ask a child to do something not developmentally appropriate for him, he will, No. 1, fail. No. 2, he will develop an aversion to the subject. By age 12, you will have girls who don't like science and boys who don't like reading...
>
> —Leonard Sax, *Why Gender Matters*[19]

Why this huge increase in reading problems among boys right around age 8? Part of the explanation is that the brain development lag is still increasing at this point, and will continue to do so for six or more years. The other part, though, has to do with how reading is being taught in schools. The end of second grade and the beginning of third grade marks a major shift in the focus of reading. Up until this point, children are still learning to read. They are being supported, working with adults, learning the nuts and bolts of a skill they are not yet expected to use. The major shift comes when they stop learning to read, and start reading to learn. Suddenly, the time to master reading is over, and the time to use it has begun. This highlights the brain lag that might have seemed unimportant just months earlier. Boys now are expected to read independently, and the teacher's focus now isn't on the skill of reading but on the content the child is expected to pick up through reading. And just to make things a bit harder, that content may be a lot more appealing to most girls than it is to most boys.

There was a huge study done in Tennessee in 2010, involving more than 1,200 kindergarteners through fifth graders. Researchers tested kids on basic skills that experts believe are necessary for learning to read. Girls entered kindergarten ahead of boys in these skills but didn't gain on boys when tested in first, second, and third grades. In fourth grade, though, boys started losing ground.[20] What does that mean? It suggests that while boys' reading itself may suffer in early school years, the basic skills are there. The way we teach the building blocks of reading probably works. It is when we stop teaching those skills, and kids need to develop them on their own, that is, third grade and on, that boys really start to suffer.

The researchers' suggestions? Look at what interests and motivates boys in the fourth grade and beyond. Specifically, consider that boys may be drawn to informational books, rather than the stories and fiction that become their regular school diet.[21] "The current results suggest that educators may want to implement procedures in fourth grade, and perhaps as early as third grade, that enhance reading fluency in males. Given that fluency may be affected by the amount one reads, educators may want to use procedures such as altering reading material, providing choices on what is read, and providing more reinforcement for reading to enhance boys' motivation to read during these grades."[22]

Boys get pushed off the dock, and it is sink or swim. This is why one-third of all American boys end up in remedial reading in the third grade. Clearly what boys need at this age—and for some years to come—is the chance to develop their reading skills at their own pace, rather than being pushed to use reading skills they don't have to acquire content. This obsession of modern schools with learning volumes of material, rather than learning how to learn, is a product of the standardized testing regime and will be addressed soon. For now what it means is that your boy is suddenly expected to read at an arbitrary level set without any consideration of his natural brain development, and he is probably going to fail.

Remedial Reading

And what happens to those boys who do fall behind at this critical stage? They end up in some form of remedial reading. The Mayo Clinic reported that boys are two to three times more likely than girls to be diagnosed with a reading disability.[23] The National Center for Education Statistics reported that boys are three to five times more likely than girls to have placements for learning or reading disabilities.[24] In 2000, 70 percent of children in all remedial classes were male.[25]

Think of what that means in the one area where boys traditionally fall behind girls, in reading. Not only does it mean a lot of boys in remedial reading, but it means they are likely to see a pattern. The only female in the room might be the teacher. Is anyone surprised that 24 percent of primary school students identify reading as a feminized activity?[26]

> Struggling readers spend so much time in remediation programs that free reading for enjoyment is limited.
> —Mary Moyer and Melissa Williams, in *Knowledge Quest*[27]

Remedial reading has always relied heavily on the teaching of skills, from understanding grammar and parts of speech to diagramming sentences and learning Greek and Latin roots. This has been magnified in recent years as high-stakes testing makes schools desperate to help more students pass the tests. These tests cannot actually measure reading ability; that isn't easily quantifiable. What they measure are skills associated with reading, and so that is what schools teach, especially in remedial reading.

Here is the problem: the eminent researcher Stephen Krashen found that becoming a reader has little to do with the acquisition of reading skills—such as vocabulary, structure, and grammar—and everything to do with volume.[28] There is no real evidence that formal language instruction produces readers. Certainly these skills make it possible for kids to read, but if that is all they get, then they have little hope of developing as readers. The only proven factor common to good readers is how much time they spent reading. Richard Allington found that students in remedial reading programs read 75 percent less than their classmates in regular reading.[29] It's a vicious circle: kids that don't read are poor readers, and poor readers read less than accomplished reads, so they never catch up.

> No matter how long students spend engaged in direct reading instruction, without time to apply what they learn in the context of real reading events, students will never build capacity as readers. Without spending increasingly longer periods of time reading, they won't build endurance as readers, either. Students need time to read and time to be readers.
> —Donalyn Miller, *The Book Whisperer*[30]

But if the research confirms that reading in volume is what makes good readers, why isn't free, student-driven reading a focus of reading programs in most schools? In 2000, the National Reading Panel, setting the theoretical foundations of No Child Left Behind, did not list independent reading as one of its recommendations for schools to focus on. In their report, they announced, "The Panel was unable to find a positive relationship between programs and instruction that encourages large amounts of independent reading and improvements in reading achievement."[31]

This is the great lie that supports so much of the damage that school curriculums inflict on children, especially boys, in the modern test-and-punish world of federal education policy. The National Reading Panel followed strict guidelines as to what research they would accept. All studies had to include a control group to compare against the results of whatever was being studied. But no sane parent would sign off on their child being in a control group that wasn't allowed to read for a year, and no responsible researcher would ask them to. The research to support independent reading is out there, and it is overwhelming. The panel simply refused to look at it.

The fact that there are no studies comparing those kids encouraged to read with those prohibited to do so just shows how obvious it is to everyone involved in education that reading in volume is beneficial. If, as the responsible research shows, independent reading is the major factor in reading progress, students who read below grade level read less than their peers, and boys are more likely to be behind in reading, then it is boys who are hurt most.

Reading for Pleasure

> [R]eading achievement has been found to be a function of the amount of time and energy students invest in reading both in and out of school.
> —Jaime L. Below et al., in *School Psychology Review*[32]

For all kids—boys and girls, those in remedial reading and those who aren't—reading in volume is the key to developing as a reader. And reading in volume means reading independently; in short, reading for pleasure. You will never read enough through school assignments to do the trick. The Organization for Economic Cooperation and Development found that pleasure reading is more important to academic success than socioeconomic status.[33] Stephen Krashen also found that the complexity of the reading kids do has little to do with how they progress as readers. So pushing kids to read at a higher level is probably counterproductive, given that most kids (like most adults) will read more if the reading is less taxing and more fun. Oddly enough, letting kids read below their grade level is most likely to make it possible to read above their grade level later on. And kids who *choose* to read harder materials will still read more than if they are *required* to read harder material.

> [L]ight reading can serve as a conduit to heavier reading: it provides both the motivation for more reading and the linguistic competence that makes harder reading possible . . . Books children select on their own are often harder than their official "reading level."
> —Stephen Krashen, *The Power of Reading*[34]

So most boys identified as being behind in reading or having reading problems are simply progressing at a different rate than their classmates because of their natural brain development. Certainly there are boys with real issues such as dyslexia and autism spectrum disorders, but for most boys, what they really need is to be allowed to read in volume at whatever level is comfortable for them while their brains develop at their own pace. If they need some added instruction to give them certain tools, then every minute of remedial instruction should earn them two more minutes of free reading time.

High-Interest/Low-Reading-Level Books

One approach to getting books in the hands of struggling readers is *hi/lo books*, meaning high interest and low reading level. These are books designed specifically to limit the challenges in reading, and such books come mostly from publishers who specialize in this form. Publishers carefully control the number of words and the complexity of those words. They make sure most of the words are common ones that readers are likely to know, even if they haven't seen them in print. They keep sentences short and uncomplicated. Likewise, they keep the books themselves short. Most important, they make sure that the reader does not need a lot of background information to understand what is going on and does not need to make a lot of inferences.

Using some pretty sophisticated formulas, publishers try to pinpoint exactly what the reading level of a book is, then try to make sure that the book is of interest to someone at least three years older than the reading level. How do you make a book more interesting to a struggling reader? Publishers look at the age of the kids in the story, assuming most kids want to read about people their age or slightly older. They also look for topics that are engaging enough to grab even those who won't read just for the sake of reading. That means a lot of edgy subject matter.

They make sure that the type size is big enough to be easy on the eye, but not so big to look babyish. They use more white space and illustrations than you would find in other books for that age group. And they make sure that plots get moving early and drive the story to a quick finish. In short, hi/lo books seem designed to appeal to boys.

So why aren't all kids' books designed this way? Anytime you design a book for a purpose other than actually telling a story, you run the risk of undercutting the story. Just think of books written obviously to make a point or drive home a moral, or those terrible stories meant to make a point about science or math. If you can see the intention behind the story, then the story is often lost.

Hi/lo books can be seen like food designed for a sick person who can't digest normal food. The ingredients you can't use, such as complex words, language, or imagery, may leave you with a bland, unsatisfying meal. Hi/lo books that are done poorly can be just awful, with short choppy sentences, obvious plots, and dialogue that sounds like baby talk. On the other hand, when done well, hi/lo books allow struggling readers to enjoy reading without all the struggles they are used to. If half the battle is convincing kids that reading can be a regular part of their lives when their skills are weak, good hi/lo books can be invaluable. There is a starter list of recent hi/lo books for guys in the last part of this book.

What Lies Ahead

You can probably guess that free reading at whatever level is comfortable is usually not the approach that schools take today. Most schools feel they can't wait for natural brain development to take place, and that producing acceptable test scores must take precedence over producing lifelong readers. The result is that by the time many boys finally catch up in brain development, they have already learned that reading is hard work, that they are bad readers, and that reading is something that comes more naturally, and so more appropriately, to girls.

Many parents of a generation ago tell stories of dragging boys through school kicking and screaming, sighing in relief as they walked across the stage to receive

Some Publishers that Specialize in Hi/Lo Books

A&D Xtreme (an imprint of ABDO Publishing Company)
www.abdopub.com

Bearport Publishing
www.bearportpublishing.com

Capstone Press (Stone Arch Books, an imprint of Capstone Press, publishes contemporary fiction)
www.capstone-press.com

High Noon Books
www.highnoonbooks.com

HIP (High Interest Publishing) Books
www.hip-books.com

Lerner Publishing
www.lernerbooks.com

Orca Book Publishers
www.orcabook.com

Saddleback Educational
www.sdlback.com

Townsend Press
www.townsendpress.com

their diploma, then bribing them to go off to college, just to try it for a semester. Then to everyone's amazement, the boy flourishes. Why? He has a brain now; that's never happened before.

Sadly, this miraculous recovery is becoming more and more rare. In my work, I am sometimes asked to help a high school boy with reading issues. The most common reaction I get from such boys is "Don't waste your time; in a few years I'll never have to read again." Either they will drop out of school or graduate. Too many boys today see high school graduation as the day they can stop reading.

Boys' post-high-school prospects are bleak and getting bleaker. Eighty percent of high school dropouts are male.[35] If that isn't bad enough, 80–90 percent of convicted felons are high school dropouts.[36] As of 2003, 72 percent of girls graduated from high school, but only 65 percent of boys.[37]

A University of Michigan study found that 62.4 percent of high school girls planned to graduate from a four-year college, to only 51.1 percent of high school boys.[38] Apparently, they meant it. American colleges today are 60 percent female.[39] In 2008, 33 percent of females ages 25–29 held a four-year degree, 26 percent of males. And those numbers are bound to get worse. The gender gap in college enrollment is increasing by one hundred thousand students a year.[40]

No Child Left Behind and the Tyranny of Standards

If it sounds like I am setting up No Child Left Behind as the great enemy of boys' reading, well, I am. Educators have long known the value of reading for pleasure, the limits of skills-based reading instruction, and the need to approach learners at the appropriate developmental level. If you are blaming teachers for the boys' reading crisis, think again. Many schools and teachers do things that hurt boy readers, and most of the time they know better, but they usually don't feel like they have a choice.

> The testing required for No Child Left Behind will cost $5.3 billion between 2002 and 2008 . . . What if that $5.3 billion were invested instead in a trust fund for school libraries, dedicated to improving both books and staffing in high poverty area schools?
> —Stephen Krashen, *The Power of Reading*[41]

People often ask me, if your approach produces better readers, why don't schools ignore all the nuts-and-bolts skills work and just let kids read? If that produces readers, then kids will do better on standardized tests. There are two answers. First, creating readers takes time, learning how to answer rigidly formatted language questions just takes learning the system. With harsh penalties looming over *this year's* scores, which approach do you think a school will take? Secondly, good readers do not necessarily do well on these tests. Remember, the tests can't measure reading—only skills associated with reading. A child can be skilled in absorbing, comprehending, and applying what he reads and still not be able to identify a subordinate clause or decode a nonsense word based on its Latin root.

Donalyn Miller contradicts the practice of teaching to the test in her amazing book aimed at teachers, *The Book Whisperer*. She points out that the standards for success on those tests are so pitifully low that good readers shouldn't have any problem passing. She teaches reading by allowing her students to drive their own reading and allowing thirty minutes of class time every day for independent reading, along with a number of other exemplary practices. Her students pass standardized tests at a dizzying rate. I won't argue with her point, just with the reality of most classrooms. If every teacher taught like she does, and every school supported their teachers in doing so, I wouldn't doubt that every child would pass any silly bubble test put in front of them. That is probably not what is happening in your boy's school.

Possibly the most devastating effect of No Child Left Behind is the narrowing of education to a single style of learning. For two decades teachers have been training in what they call *differentiated instruction*, which means teaching in different ways to better match the different learning styles of their students. In the late 1990s, teachers were just starting to develop ways of assessing students in different ways to better gauge what they had actually learned, an idea known as *differentiated assessment*. No Child Left Behind, with its single way of testing students to get a number that can be compared across schools, states, and the country, put an end to all of that. If there is one way to test kids, then there is one way to teach them, and if your son doesn't happen to learn or test well in that particular way, then he is in for trouble. As it turns out, boys tend to be experiential learners, and that does not fit the one-size-fits-all approach. No Child Left Behind was designed to leave large numbers of children behind, and boys figure prominently.

> Teaching to increase state standards and national achievement scores frustrates teachers, fails students, and places erroneous and erratic pressures on education. When school systems use a generic prescription to suit all students across the board, individual learning styles are cheated and creativity is stifled.
> —Alison Follos, school librarian, *Reviving Reading*[42]

Canned Reading

But the No Child Left Behind legislation has a greater effect than differentiated assessment because it has set up a culture of standards that affects every aspect of education. High-stakes testing promises to reduce the academic progress of a student, a class, or a school to a single number—a ridiculous idea when you look at it. Schools and teachers are judged on their ability to produce students who can answer disconnected questions at an arbitrary level of accuracy under artificial time pressure, a skill not likely to benefit them in the modern workforce. Schools constrict the curriculum and the way they teach to accommodate this narrow approach to assessment.

Teaching reading becomes a mechanical activity, spawning canned reading programs that companies produce and schools adopt in their entirety. Schools spend thousands upon thousands of dollars on these programs, and teachers spend thousands of hours learning and implementing them. In poor districts especially, strapped for cash and understaffed, there may be no resources left over to do any other kind of reading instruction. Teaching reading becomes the educational equivalent of ordering a Happy Meal: standardized, mass produced, and delivered in a neat little box.

> [T]here was no evidence that [reading management programs] improved reading achievement or attitudes toward reading.
> —Stephen Krashen, *The Power of Reading*[43]

The most prevalent of these canned reading programs is Accelerated Reader (AR), though it is just one of many. It is instructive to look at because it shows the position schools, students, and parents get put in when standards rule education. The theory behind AR is actually quite good, and especially well suited to many boys. The idea is to get kids to read in volume by offering a huge range of reading that the student himself can select from. If there are books that aren't in the program that a teacher wants to use, she can simply add them by writing up a simple assessment test for each. Reading at any level is honored because points are awarded based on the complexity of the book, so you can earn ten points by reading five books at a simple two-point level, or two books at a higher five-point level. Testing is standardized, sure, but it is very simple and done by computer, which seems to have some appeal.

So far, so good, but AR has fallen apart at the implementation at most schools that I have observed. First, the range of books initially offered through the program was woefully inadequate. There were a lot of titles, but they were mostly older and the types of books usually offered through school reading programs, which meant not nearly enough in the genres and virtually no nonfiction. (More on the types of reading with broad boy appeal later.) This is improving rapidly, but schools that adopted AR early have been behind in book choice for years. The option of teachers adding books on their own is a great idea, but it proved impractical in most cases. Teachers simply don't have the time. Instead of using AR to supplement a reading curriculum, as it was intended, underfunded and understaffed schools adopted it as their de facto reading curriculum. There was little time and few resources set aside for anything other than implementing the program and keeping it running.

The fatal blow, though, came when so many schools immediately abandoned the idea of letting kids read at any level and honoring that reading. The first thing too many schools did was restrict students to reading books within one year of their grade-level reading. That cut the heart out of a well-thought-out program and put boys back in the grade-level-reading trap. They were expected to read at a developmentally inappropriate level, when what they needed to do was read in volume at a lower level to catch up.

Researcher Teri S. Lesesne reported on her own family's struggle with AR. She and her daughters realized that success in AR—gaining more points and doing better on the computerized tests—leads to an automatic raising of the levels of books to be read. In short, readers are punished with a "push" for doing well. The answer? A reading expert had to advise her own daughter to limit herself to reporting only that she read the number of books required.[44]

In the spirit of full disclosure, I should point out that as I write this, I am currently writing original books for one of these canned reading programs (not Accelerated Reader). How did that happen? The editor who contacted me started her pitch with, "I know you don't believe in this, but . . ." then went on to explain that whether I agreed with the approach or not, schools are using these programs and the kids deserve something good to read. This particular program creates original books that are included in the "box," but the books being produced for fourth through sixth graders lacked a lot of boy appeal, just as the initial AR list had. That was where I came in.

This sales pitch tells a great deal about how parents can approach this tyranny of standards in American education today. Parents cannot change the law—at least, not individually and in the short run—and probably cannot change the way their sons' schools deal with it. But they can recognize what is going on, understand where the approach fails, and try to support boys' reading in whatever ways are within their power.

Illogical Extremes

How far does this tyranny of standards reach? Boys are four and a half times more likely than girls to be expelled from preschool, largely due to the more academic focus of preschools today.[45] My mind screeches to a halt at the idea of an expellable offense in preschool. Have we become so obsessed with measurable benchmarks that we have ruined the creative growth experience of preschool? Eventually, this regime must so overstep the bounds of good sense that we will see it for the sham that it is. I thought that moment had come in the spring of 2012, but I was wrong.

I was due to speak to the Rotary Club in Exeter, New Hampshire, when I heard that the Oyster River Middle School (ORMS) in Durham, New Hampshire, had just made the watch list for No Child Left Behind.[46] The school had failed to make adequate progress on standardized tests, and if it didn't reverse the trend, it faced sanctions. ORMS is a well-supported school located in the same town as the University of New Hampshire. Students tend to come from well-educated and involved parents. The school benefits from students in the university's education department researching and investigating cutting-edge educational practices. I had been involved in a number of initiatives in the school and knew it to be a vibrant learning community. The idea that somehow it was failing under No Child Left Behind struck me as the equivalent of Joe McCarthy going after Eisenhower. Surely this was the absurd step that would expose the whole ridiculous approach.

I said as much to the Rotary Club in Exeter, home of Philips Exeter Academy and in many ways a similarly education-rich town. I was amazed when an audience member asked how I could defend a school that cost so much in tax money but still failed. As a speaker, I feel pretty confident I can hold my own in a question-and-answer period, but this one threw me and I missed the chance to make the obvious reply. What makes you say ORMS was failing? A standardized test that promises to reduce education to a single number? An educational approach dictated from a federal agency that tells teachers in every diverse community in America the one best way for their students to learn?

Seeing an obviously exemplary school run afoul of No Child Left Behind should have been proof of the program's flawed basis. Instead, this man, who knew his local school, rejected the evidence of his own experience and accepted a dictate from some alien power that ORMS should conform rather than continue to serve its students. Sadly, the principal of the school immediately announced that the school would make changes to how they taught in order to meet the federal standards.

If you are worried that your son is not succeeding because of his scores on some multiple choice bubble test, don't be. The test does not, and cannot, test his reading ability. What it tests and how it tests bears no relation to what will make him successful as a reader or in life. Many even question whether a majority of boys try on these tests. If boys are concrete learners, then exerting themselves on a meaningless assessment would seem pointless. What you should be worried about is the time and energy wasted on preparing for these tests, and the stress and feelings of inadequacy that are bound to follow.

Recognize what boys really need to become readers. As a parent, you need to realize that the only way for boys to become readers is to read in volume and to develop the habit of reading for their own pleasure. The biggest obstacles to boys who do not read independently revolve around choice. Boys often don't feel they have a choice in the types of reading they do—as will be discussed in a little while—and they feel like they are being forced to read at a certain level. Schools will not carve out room for choice in a world where even the best schools face a loss of resources and independence if they don't herd students into an educational cattle chute. You need to provide the space to become a reader, and how you do that is what the rest of this book is about.

Big Question: Phonics or Whole Language?

If the question is, should schools use a phonics or whole language approach to teach reading, the answer is yes. Every student needs some of each, and every child will need a different balance to be most successful. The argument that too many educators engage in between the two philosophies—and even the arguments about how much of each is best—ultimately hurts your boy. Any attempt to dictate an answer ignores the fact that there is no right approach, and limits the freedom of the teacher to adjust to the specific needs of the class or, better still, the individual student.

Phonics-based language instruction was originally trumpeted as a boy-friendly approach. The antiphonics backlash is based largely on the fact that phonics programs sometimes try to edge out all other approaches, leading to dull, canned reading programs that leave no room for children to practice the skills they acquire. Ideally, you should fight for the teachers who work with your boy to have the independence and training to teach in a way that makes sense. Failing that, be aware of what system your school uses and provide what is missing. There are phonics systems available in the retail market, as well as any number of private tutoring programs that offer phonics help. If your school goes overboard on the side of phonics, then library programs and book clubs are your best antidote, as will be discussed later.

NOTES

1. Jon Scieszka, "Guys and Reading," *Teacher Librarian*, February 2003, 17.

2. Richard Whitmire, "Boy Trouble," *New Republic*, January 23, 2006, 18.

3. Sean Fine, "Schools Told to Fix Boys' Low Grades," *Globe and Mail*, August 27, 2001, http://v1.theglobeandmail.com/series/school/fix.html.

4. James M. Royer and Rachel E. Wing, "Making Sense of Sex Differences in Reading and Math Assessment: The Practice and Engagement Hypothesis," *Issues in Education*, 2002, 77.

5. Peg Tyre, *The Trouble with Boys: A Surprising Report Card on Our Sons, Their Problems at School, and What Parents and Educators Must Do* (Crown Publishers, 2008), 65.

6. Amanda Ripley, "Who Says a Woman Can't Be Einstein?" *Time*, March 7, 2005, 55.

7. Michael Gurian and Patricia Henley, with Terry Trueman, *Boys and Girls Learn Differently! A Guide for Teachers and Parents* (Jossey-Bass, 2001), 56.

8. Whitmire, "Boy Trouble," 15.

9. Gurian and Henley, *Boys and Girls Learn Differently*, 37.

10. Doreen Kimura, "Sex Differences in the Brain," *Scientific American*, September 1992, 27.

11. Leonard Sax, *Why Gender Matters: What Parents and Teachers Need to Know about the Emerging Science of Sex Differences* (Doubleday, 2005), 94–95.

12. Tyre, *The Trouble with Boys*, 94.

13. Leonard Sax, *Boys Adrift: The Five Factors Driving the Growing Epidemic of Unmotivated Boys and Underachieving Young Men* (Basic Books, 2007), 20–21.

14. Tyre, *The Trouble with Boys*, 27.

15. Ibid., 28.

16. Christine Robinson, "A Developmental Difference," *Casper Star Tribune*, August 1, 2007, http://trib.com/news/article_d80a9c9d-e083-53f9-8811-6a3037ac5bb1.html.

17. Fairbanks North Star Borough Public Library, *Guys Read Pilot Program: Final Report* (2007), 1.

18. Richard Whitmire, *Why Boys Fail: Saving Our Sons from an Educational System That's Leaving Them Behind* (American Management Association, 2010), 32.

19. Quoted in Ripley, "Who Says a Woman Can't Be Einstein?" 56.

20. Jaime L. Below et al., "Gender Differences in Early Literacy: Analysis of Kindergarten through Fifth-Grade Dynamic Indicators of Basic Early Literacy Skills Probes," *School Psychology Review*, 2010, 252.

21. Ibid., 252–53.

22. Ibid., 254.

23. Whitmire, "Boy Trouble," 15.

24. Josephine Peyton Young and William G. Brozo, "Boys Will Be Boys, or Will They? Literacy and Masculinities," *Reading Research Quarterly*, July/August/September 2001, 318.

25. Stan Steiner, "Where Have All the Men Gone? Male Role Models in the Reading Crisis," *PNLA Quarterly*, Summer 2000, 17.

26. Pamela J. Farris et al., "Male Call: Fifth-Grade Boys' Reading Preferences," *Reading Teacher*, November 2009, 180.

27. Mary Moyer and Melissa Williams, "Personal Programming," *Knowledge Quest*, March/April 2011, 69.

28. Stephen D. Krashen, *The Power of Reading: Insights from the Research*, 2nd ed. (Libraries Unlimited, 2004), 116.

29. Donalyn Miller, *The Book Whisperer* (Jossey-Bass, 2009), 25.

30. Ibid., 51.

31. Ibid., 3.

32. Below et al., "Gender Differences in Early Literacy," 241.

33. Christina Clark and Kate Rumbold, *Reading for Pleasure: A Research Overview* (National Literacy Trust, 2006), 6.

34. Krashen, *The Power of Reading*, 116.

35. Whitmire, "Boy Trouble," 15.

36. Aaron Kipnis, *Angry Young Men: How Parents, Teachers, and Counselors Can Help "Bad Boys" Become Good Men* (Jossey-Bass, 2002), 55.

37. J. Greene and M. Winters, *Leaving Boys Behind: Public High School Graduation Rates* (Manhattan Institute, 2006), www.manhattan-institute.org/html/cr_48.htm.

38. Whitmire, "Boy Trouble," 16.

39. Gurian and Henley, *Boys and Girls Learn Differently*, 56.

40. Tyre, *The Trouble with Boys*, 32.

41. Krashen, *The Power of Reading*, 77.

42. Alison M. G. Follos, *Reviving Reading: School Library Programming, Author Visits and Books That Rock!* (Libraries Unlimited, 2006), 14.

43. Krashen, *The Power of Reading*, 119.

44. Lesesne, *Naked Reading*, 16.

45. Whitmire, *Why Boys Fail*, 3.

46. Michael Winerip, "In a Standardized Era, a Creative School Is Forced to Be More So," *New York Times*, October 30, 2011, www.nytimes.com/2011/10/31/education/no-child-left-behind-catches-up-with-new-hampshire-school.html.

Why Boys Read

Big Question: Nature or Nurture?

It may seem strange to ask why boys would read. After all, aren't kids supposed to read for the joy of reading? Sure, some just love getting lost in a book, but fewer than we would like to think, and fewer of those are boys than girls. Even if kids find some pleasure in the act of reading itself, most also read for a purpose. When that purpose is to fulfill a requirement—either for school or an anxious parent who makes a child get a book to read—pleasure really doesn't play into it. But sometimes even a child who has been turned off from the act of reading itself will read to fill some psychological need.

Here is your inspirational thought of the day: children read to become better adults. Children—or lion cubs, for that matter—work out roles and skills they will need when they grow up during play. Cubs practice fighting, stalking, and dominance and submission practices. Children act out future professions, conflict resolution, and methods of determining social standing. In the same way, children explore the ways they will interact with the world in their reading.[1] Why, then, do girls so often dive into reading more avidly than boys? Largely because the adults in their lives do not understand what boys need from their reading. We see reading the way girls are likely to see reading, and we fail to connect with boys.

The most basic difference between the average boy and the average girl is in outlook. The average girl tends to internalize; the average boy tends to externalize.[2] That means that a girl will see a big, wide, wonderful world and think, "Everything out there is reflected in me. If there is goodness in the world, then there must be goodness in me. If there is evil in the world, then there must be evil in me." Girls feel connected to the world around them. It is what makes them able to feel sympathy and empathy. It is what allows them to see a puppy suffering and feel its pain.

Boys are more likely to be causing the puppy the pain, and there is a reason for that. Boys will see a big, wide, interesting world and think, "If I don't get out there soon, it will pass me by." They don't feel that connection with the world, and they crave it. This is why so many boys are experiential learners. If they can't feel and touch, if they can't get their hands dirty, then they just don't care because they just don't connect. Girls look for the universal in themselves; boys look for themselves in the universe.

This view helps explain what researcher Leonard Sax confirms, and what most of us know instinctively: that boys are far more likely to engage in risky behavior. They are more likely to be injured or even killed in accidents involving bicycles, firearms, or drowning. What's more, this greater tendency toward risky behavior appears too early in life to be completely explained through socialization.[3] We have all seen this tendency, much more prevalent in boys than in girls, to put one's self in mortal physical and psychological danger on a regular basis. It is just barbaric, but it isn't inexplicable.

Boys' disconnected worldviews probably explain much of this risky behavior. The basic idea goes that if you ask a boy he can tell you: if someone were to take his bike to the roof of the school and ride it off, he would probably get hurt. The boy gets that. Now, what will that boy do since you put the idea in his head? He himself will take his bike to the roof of the school and ride it off, because the fact that someone else would get hurt has no effect on him. He thinks, "The only way to know what would happen to me is to try it myself."

Still sounds a bit theoretical? Well, psychology becomes reality at the point of motivation. Everyone wants to do good in this world—children probably more so than adults, being less cynical in general. But how you do good in the world depends on how you see the world operating. Girls—feeling connected to the world around them—when confronted with a problem are more likely to seek help than to dive into the fray on their own. They believe the world works on cooperation and communication. The way to solve a problem is to get people together, agree on the problem, agree on a solution, and work together to solve the problem.

Boys, feeling more disconnected, are likely to take what one participant in a seminar I gave some years ago gleefully called "the Home Depot approach to life." Rules and tools—that is how boys tend to approach problems. Help me understand how the world works, why the problem exists in the first place, and how I can manipulate things to make them better. This difference in how children see the world operating goes a long way toward explaining why boys spend two-thirds of their playtime in competitive games, while girls spend two-thirds of their playtime in cooperative play.[4]

Of course, these traits are just generalities. All kids are unique, but these trends are common enough to show us that they can explain the behavior of many, many children. If they look eerily familiar to some adults, it may be because they are lifelong traits. We never really grow out of them. And if much of this reminds you of the adults you know, remember that children are psychological purists. They haven't undergone the mellowing process of experience. Psychologically, children are what they will be as adults, only more so.

Now what does all this psychological theory have to do with reading? Simply put, girls will tend to read to help them understand cooperation and communication. The most important aspect of a book is likely to be the characters. They will read for subtlety and practice understanding the meaning behind words and actions. Take a look at a book club edition of a literary work—say, something from Oprah's Book Club. Look at the discussion questions in the back. It won't take long to recognize that most of the questions focus on issues of interpersonal relations. Then remember who the target audience is. If this is how adult women read, it will be how girls read as well.

> Women constantly seek information about relationships because we're programmed for it. It's our psychological "job." So for many women, even those of us who also read professional and job related books, fiction is information. It analyzes human relationships and in so doing provides training for the job of being a successful female.
>
> —Carol Hole, in *American Libraries*[5]

Boys tend to read to understand the world around them. They look first for how actions affect the people and events. In short, they will read for plot. Things that obscure or inhibit the motion of the plot distract and annoy a number of boys. Of course, men tend to read the same way.

These very different ways of looking at reading mean that we can completely misread how kids approach books. Literature experts often talk about kids reading for two disparate reasons, among others. Kids may read for escapism, getting lost in a good book, or autobiographically, trying to find clues to their own lives in reading that mirrors their own situations.[6] Hence a girl is likely to get lost in a historical romance one day and pick up a gritty urban novel the next to explore how she might deal with a schoolyard bully that has been bothering her.

But boys may blur this line more than most of us realize. Because they tend to be externalists, many boys do not want to tackle personal issues so directly. They prefer to examine their lives at arm's length. So they are more likely to turn to what is generally considered escapist literature, most notably fantasy, to read autobiographically. How can a boy see himself in a story full of dragons and ogres? Because he is more comfortable looking at life from the outside. The gritty urban novel may be the perfect choice so long as he isn't dealing with any of the issues in the book. You don't want to dismiss what looks like escapist literature too quickly until you see it through your boy's eyes.

Boy Readers, Boy Explorers

The difference between boys' and girls' outlooks can explain why so much of what boys read is so edgy. The humor is gross and borderline antisocial, the informational books are disgusting, the action and fantasy books are violent, the gothic horror is so dark, and there is entirely too much discussion of bodily functions. Why do boys have to love the books that drive us crazy?

Because they drive us crazy—that's the point. Boys need to push limits. Their disconnected view of the world makes them eager to head out and explore. But explorers do not want to explore the center of the map; somebody has already been there. Do you remember what they used to write on the edges of maps back when they didn't know what lay beyond? "Here be monsters." They didn't write that to discourage exploration; they did it to make sure someone would go look, and that someone was usually male.

So just like boys will tend to take more physical risks, they are more likely to go into dangerous territory reading. This has led to the questionable assumption that boys read edgy material and then act it out. While this thought may be annoying when you are talking about making rude noises at the dinner table after reading *Captain Underpants*, it gets more serious when you start talking about the violence in some kids' books.

Some parents worry, when their boy is drawn toward books with violent themes, that this is a reflection of a violent nature in their boy—or worse, that their boy is learning to be violent through his reading. In most cases, neither of these assumptions is true. You have to remember that boys often explore their world through reading. Specifically, they read about things they do not understand.

[I]n a society in which children are exposed to violent images in their environment from an early age, war play can serve as an important vehicle through which children can work on the thoughts and feelings they have about the violence they see around them.
—Nancy Carlsson-Paige and Diane E. Levin, *Who's Calling the Shots?*[7]

When I worked as a public librarian next door to an elementary school, there was a fifth-grade teacher who would call me up every time there was a school shooting in the news and ask me to "booktalk" to her kids. *Booktalking* is a librarian's term for giving short sales pitches for books so that children can have a new set of books to choose from. Whenever I received this call, I knew what the teacher wanted. I would come into her class and she would excuse herself to go get a cup of coffee.

I would spend twenty minutes sharing a pile of great books with her kids, and finish with the book *Give a Boy a Gun* by Todd Strasser. It is a great book about a fictional Columbine-style event. It gets into the heads of two desperate, marginalized teenagers who feel they have no choice but to enter their school with weapons. For kids—and boys especially—confused about headlines of such a heinous act, it offers a safe, arms-reach opportunity to think and understand. It is also just the kind of book that a middle school teacher would be hard-pressed to defend having in her classroom library in today's violence-conscious world. Hence, call in the librarian . . . and if someone complains, the teacher has some distance to protect herself.

I was glad the teacher was aware enough to call me in for this much needed service, but frustrated that such a ruse was necessary. We need to recognize why boys so often are drawn to such edgy books, and why such books are in some ways necessary. Being explorers, boys will seek out information on things in their world they do not understand. That means violence, sex, drugs, hatred, and more that will make their parents uncomfortable. However, they won't seek these things out because they like them, but because these things don't fit in their worldview.

Yes, there are tough situations that boys grow up in, but by and large we have created safe environments for children in our society. Children are certainly more protected here than in many parts of the world, and are more protected than children were even one or two generations ago in this society. When boys see violence on the evening news, they will seek out sources of information on it because for the most part, our boys grow up with little actual experience of violence. (Thank goodness for that.) The question is, where will they get their information?

Another gender issue that stands out in the data is the difference in the percent of boys vs. girls who have imitated aggressive behaviors they saw on TV (45% of boys compared to 28% of girls). This difference is especially pronounced among the four- to six-year-olds (59% of boys vs. 35% of girls).

—Kaiser Family Foundation, *Zero to Six*[8]

The first answer—the one that you thought of as soon as you read that boys have little actual experience with violence—is the media. Yes, our boys have plenty of experience with violence in television, movies, and video games. A Kaiser Family Foundation survey found that the average American child spends six and a half hours *per day* watching television, using computers, or engaged in other electronic activities.[9] Douglas A. Gentile, an Iowa State University psychologist, reported that among third- to fifth-grade rural and suburban kids, girls play video games six hours per week and boys thirteen hours per week.[10] Avid 13-year-old television watchers witness seven thousand screen murders in a given year.[11] Is that where you want your boy solely learning about violence?

The media handles violence terribly. Words do not translate well to the screen, so violence usually overshadows communication. There is little time to work out problems when all problems must be solved in thirty minutes, an hour, or two hours. That means there are no long-term consequences—because there is no long term. Keep in mind the television cartoon *South Park*. For many years, the show always ended with a character dying. And not a different character, but the same one week after week. Kenny dies every week on *South Park*. And then the next week he is back, no explanation given. There is no better proof that long-term consequences don't exist in the media.

Especially with boys, I think letting them read books that are provocative or borderline appropriate . . . is motivating. What draws middle school and high school boys to the edgy themes of certain movies and video games, the visceral imagery, the suggestive scenes, the subversive tone can be found in young adult books; they just don't know it.

—Donalyn Miller, *The Book Whisperer*[12]

The other way boys are likely to explore edgy subjects is in their own lives through experience. Remember the boy who rides his bike off the roof to see if he will get hurt? Except in certain environments where social and economic factors make destructive behavior endemic, boys play at fighting, experiment with controlled substances, and engage in early sexual behaviors because they want to know. Often the media gives an incomplete and unsatisfactory explanation of these things, only prompting more experimentation. Is that how you want your boy learning the ropes?

Obviously, reading is a better way for boys to explore the ragged edges of their world. Books offer time for problems to be worked out and for consequences of actions to be realized. Books use language to make the complexity of situations apparent. And best of all, nobody ends up bleeding. Answering a similar question about violence in children's play, Nancy Carlsson-Paige and Diane E. Levin point out that "it does children a disservice to cut them off from a form of play that is well-suited to help them work through their thoughts and feelings about the increasing amounts of violence they see."[13]

Honoring the Why of Boys' Reading

I spent a week of lunch periods reading to fourth, fifth, and sixth graders at the Greenland Central School in Greenland, New Hampshire, in a program called Literary Lunch. The idea was that one reader would come in for five days and read an entire book to a group of about twenty-five students; no tests, no reports, just sit back and enjoy someone reading you a book. The power of the approach was probably best shown by the fact that while I was reading to the kids sitting at desks eating their lunches, adults lined the walls of the room. Everybody loves a good story.

I was reading a favorite book of mine, *Swear to Howdy*, by Wendelin Van Draanen. For Monday's session through Wednesday's, it was the funniest book most of the listeners—kids and adults—had ever heard. I literally had kids fall out of their seats laughing. It is a wonderful story of two boys who meet up in a small southern town at the beginning of a summer and just spend the summer being boys. They torment their sisters, catch a ten-pound bullfrog they name Tank, and rig up a ghost on a pulley to drop on unsuspecting pedestrians.

Then, during Thursday's reading, the book took an extremely serious turn. The boys' fake ghost falls on a car windshield and the car crashes, killing the driver, who happens to be one of the boys' sisters. By Friday, the distraught brother puts the business end of a shotgun in his mouth (he does *not* pull the trigger). The adults around the room went from worried to frantically signaling for me to stop reading. Oddly, not a single student showed the least concern.

It is a wonderful story about consequences and friendship through thick and thin. It is also the kind of edgy story that makes adults very uncomfortable. I think the fact that it starts as such a funny story probably made it even harder for the adults to accept. But here is why it was important to read it: At the end of the program two boys approached me. One of them thanked me for reading the book, saying he could not think of another adult who would have dared.

Later in this book we will get to the types of reading boys often enjoy, as well as some lists of books to put in boys' hands, but for now remember the why. Boys' outlook tends to make them explorers. They are more interested in how the world works and how their actions will affect outcomes. They are doers and explorers. They will focus less on the interactions of characters in their reading, because they focus less on cooperation and communication than girls do. We often look at reading from a more female perspective, probably because it is most often women who teach reading and set the standards for literature, something we will also explore in more detail later.

We need to recognize that boys' views of reading often differ from that of adults, namely teachers and parents. This goes a long way toward explaining why boys in general do not succeed as well at reading as girls do. And always remember that this doesn't make boys wrong. They read for reasons that satisfy their needs. We just don't always see their needs the way they do. The motivation for boys to read will affect how they read and what they read. The next chapter will address the how.

Big Question: Nature or Nurture?

Nature or nurture? It is a question that comes up just about everywhere and every time I speak with parents about boys and reading. Sure, boys on average don't read as much or as well as girls, but is that because of something physical in the makeup of boys (nature)? Or is it because we treat boys and girls differently (nurture)? Boys act differently than girls, but is it the way they are hardwired, or the way they are raised? If the whole question seems too academic, then you might want to skip to the start of the next chapter. But if the question sparks something, well, here are a few thoughts on the matter.

It is sort of a one-sided question. Not too many people question that social forces affect how children act and how they learn. In the Girl Power movement of the 1970s and 1980s, we found out that girls were falling behind boys in math and science, but quickly realized that this had much more to do with how we taught these subjects than it did any difference in abilities. We changed how we taught these subjects, sometimes even creating all-girl math and science classes, and used social pressure in a positive way. We ran ad campaigns promoting math and science as career paths for girls, and we offered special scholarships for women to study these fields at top universities. Within less than two generations, the math and science gaps in American high schools have all but disappeared.

So it isn't hard for modern educators to see that there is a social component to the boys' reading problem. Funny, though, we see it not as a problem in education that needs to be addressed, but a problem in boys themselves. As one education journal in Australia puts it:

> Feminists, on the other hand, have rejected the boys as disadvantaged thesis and stressed the importance of a "which boys?/which girls?" approach . . . in particular, a focus on quality classroom and schooling practices that problematise and seek to decrease the gender differentiated behaviours and expectations that constrain academic success.
> —Amanda Keddie, *Gender and Education*[14]

What does all that edu-speak mean? It means that boys don't succeed because they do things, and fail to do things, that hurt their achievement. Boys aren't born to be poor readers—they choose to be and they are taught to be. If that sounds a bit extreme, there is good reason for some educators to make the argument. We fought hard to make schools more welcoming and hospitable to girls, and if we decide that the resulting schools are inhospitable to boys, we could lose some or all of that valuable ground we won. No sensible person would want to turn back the clock on girls' education.

That of course is an oversimplified version of the argument, but the argument itself is a broad stroke that doesn't really play out in reality. The failure of boys in reading is so broad, so consistent, and so long-standing that it is hard to say that so many boys have so consistently proved to be lazy, entitled, and uncaring about their reading. Yes, there are social factors that hurt boys' reading, but some of those factors are beyond boys' control.

And social factors alone cannot explain the difference between boys' and girls' and their reading success. Nancy Carlsson-Paige and Diane E. Levin observed that children become gender aware at around 18 months.[15] Jonathan Gottschall reports that children engage in gender-specific play as early as 7 months.[16] That really appears to be too early for nurture to have had much effect yet. The idea that the only difference between boys and girls is that some fool put a pink bonnet on one and a blue bonnet on the other way back in the nursery, and we taught them to act accordingly, just doesn't hold water. Boys don't grow up the way they do entirely because they got toy guns for their birthday, and girls don't grow up the way they do entirely because they were given dolls.

International statistics show that the boys' reading problem is clearly not one just of our culture and our educational system. Girls outperformed boys in every country that participated in the 2003 Programme for International Student Assessment (PISA) study.[17] Stephen Gorard, education professor at the University of York in England, studied the reading scores in twenty-two countries. Boys' reading scores lagged behind in every one.[18] While how we approach reading matters, there are clearly biological factors in play as well. Boys' reading problems are a matter of both nature and nurture.

――――

NOTES

1. Jonathan Gottschall, *The Storytelling Animal: How Stories Make Us Human* (Houghton Mifflin, 2012), 41.

2. Eva M. Pomerantz, Ellen Rydell Altermatt, and Jill L. Saxon, "Making the Grade but Feeling Distressed: Gender Differences in Academic Performance and Internal Distress," *Journal of Educational Psychology*, June 2002, 396–404.

3. Leonard Sax, *Why Gender Matters: What Parents and Teachers Need to Know about the Emerging Science of Sex Differences* (Doubleday, 2005), 41–42.

4. Louann Brizendine, *The Male Brain* (Broadway Books, 2010), 18.

5. Carol Hole, "Click! The Feminization of the Public Library: Policies and Attitudes Make Men the Great Unserved," *American Libraries*, December 1990, 1079.

6. Lesesne, *Naked Reading*, 18.

7. Nancy Carlsson-Paige and Diane E. Levin, *Who's Calling the Shots? How to Respond Effectively to Children's Fascination with War Play, War Toys and Violent TV* (New Society Publishers, 1990), 31.

8. Victoria J. Rideout, Elizabeth A. Vandewater, and Ellen A. Wartella, *Zero to Six: Electronic Media in the Lives of Infants, Toddlers and Preschoolers* (Henry J. Kaiser Family Foundation, 2003), 11.

9. Marilyn Elias, "Electronic World Swallows Up Kids' Time, Study Finds," *USA Today*, March 10, 2005, A.1.

10. Tyre, *The Trouble with Boys*, 189.

11. Follos, *Reviving Reading*, 11.

12. Miller, *The Book Whisperer*, 86.

13. Carlsson-Paige and Levin, *Who's Calling the Shots*, 3.

14. Amanda Keddie, "Feminist Struggles to Mobilise Progressive Spaces within the 'Boy-Turn' in Gender Equity and Schooling Reform," *Gender and Education*, July 2010, 354.

15. Carlsson-Paige and Levin, *Who's Calling the Shots*, 95.

16. Gottschall, *The Storytelling Animal*, 39.

17. William G. Brozo, "Gender and Reading Literacy," *Reading Today*, February/March 2005, 18.

18. Valerie Strauss, "Educators Differ on Why Boys Lag in Reading," *Washington Post*, March 15, 2005, A12.

How Boys Read

Big Question: Are E-readers the Answer?

If sometimes boys and girls seem to be different species, then the human genome project has some good news for you: you aren't crazy. Human males share slightly more genes with male chimpanzees than they do with human females.[1] All right, that says more about how our DNA works than about how *we* work, but it is worth reminding ourselves that there are differences between boys and girls, and sometimes you just have to laugh about it.

The main reason that laughter is needed is because boys' reading involves so much stress. Teachers stress about the lack of progress in so many boys, and often they stress about all boys, even the ones who do read well. They transmit this stress to parents, who probably are stressed enough on their own. Everyone transfers that stress to boys either through pressure or obvious hand-wringing.

Sometimes we fail to see the signs of stress in a boy, often because our own stress clouds our judgment, and we misread his behavior as obstinacy, laziness, or lack of focus. This is a classic negative feedback loop. The only way to break it is to step back and see clearly what is going on so that we can act in a way that helps, rather than react in a way that continues the cycle.

Be aware of the signs of stress in a boy's reading life. As a public children's librarian, I was used to seeing the classic confrontation between parent and son. They would come in and Mom insists that Junior gets a book in a tone that makes it clear that this is a regular battle. Junior insists he doesn't want a book, and when pressed chooses a tiny paperback that appalls Mom. The book is likely well below the boy's grade level; is objectionably funny, silly, or gross; is part of an endless series that the boy seems addicted to; and may in fact be a book he has read many times before. Sound familiar?

What is happening here is called *regression*. Regression is a stress reaction. All organisms, when they are stressed, step back to an earlier stage to regroup, reenergize, and come back stronger. Think about bulbs that are cut back, rest, are replanted, and bloom again. Psychologically people do the same thing, and the boy described above is showing every sign of regression. This experience is probably most common with boys ages 8 to 12, in that period after they are expected to become independent readers and their reading scores plummet, the "tipping point" discussed already. Reading books over and over again, reading only in series, reading below grade level, and focusing on the kind of humor that is well younger than him—these are all signs of going back to an earlier time. That earlier time was probably the last time he enjoyed reading.

So the boy is feeling stressed about his reading; how is his reaction? Actually, there really isn't anything wrong with it. There is nothing wrong with regressing in your reading. Adults do it all the time when they go back to the same, formulaic author, reread favorite books, and even pull out a book from their childhood. We just don't see it as healthy in children, especially if the child is behind in reading or being resistant to reading. We are already stressed, so we worry creating more stress. Step back and realize that this is a phase that will pass when the boy feels more confident. Meanwhile, just the time spent reading will help his abilities, and if he enjoys the experience it will raise his confidence.

Active Readers, Active Reading

One of the basic differences between boys and girls that we can actually observe is in the way their brains are structured. By now most people have heard about how one half of the brain controls creativity and the other controls the ability to analyze. You may have even heard that boys tend to work slightly more on the analytical side of the brain.

The differences here are minimal enough that most parents need not care, but there is another structure in the brain that has a powerful influence on boys.

It is called the *corpus callosum*, and it controls the communication between the two halves of the brain. It is in effect the traffic cop of the brain. It is also 10 percent or more larger in the average girl than it is in the average boy, and far more active.[2] That difference does not disappear as we age; the same discrepancy exists between the brains of adult men and women.

What does that difference mean in everyday terms? It means when boys approach a new problem, they are likely to do so using either creativity or analysis. Girls will take a more holistic approach, using both creativity and analysis. If you were to peek at a brain scan of the two, the boy's brain would show a lot of energy being used in one half of his brain, and the girl's brain would show the energy more evenly distributed across her brain.

Most of the time, this makes little difference. We don't need our entire brains to do much. But there are some tasks that do require both halves of the brain, and language is one of them.[3] The language centers of the brain are scattered across both hemispheres. This means that girls do have a natural advantage when it comes to language. But this can be overcome; in fact every boy knows instinctively how to overcome this difference.

When the brain is asked to do something it isn't ready to do, it tends to fall asleep, and the body soon follows. At these times, boys will seek out stimuli in their environment to wake up the brain and make it work more efficiently. It is similar to kick-starting a motorcycle: add some energy up front, and the motor takes over from there. What do I mean by stimuli in the environment? Sound, color, motion, and physical activity. Does that sound like your boy when you sit him down to read or do his homework?

Parents often become concerned when their sons want to play music, stare out a window, or bounce a ball when they should be reading. We think of these things as distractions, when they are really attempts to wake up the brain and make it better prepared to deal with language. The language they are expected to deal with is often way above what they are developmentally ready for. Relax—your son is on the right track. Think about how many fathers sit down with the newspaper in front of the TV news. Many women cannot believe they can read with all that background noise, but the fact of the matter is, that is the only way they *can* read.

And if it seems that boys require a great deal more stimuli than girls do, remember that girls' brains are further developed than their male counterparts of the same age, so the reading they are being asked to do is probably not as hard for them. Also, girls are much better at picking up stimuli from their environment.

Girls are six times more likely to be able to sing in tune, which has less to do with your voice than your ear.[4] If you can hear distinctions in sound, you are more likely to be able to sing well. Girls see color better than boys do.[5] Girls smell better than boys, and in this case I am referring to their ability to distinguish smells, not emit them.[6]

This idea that boys pick up less stimuli from their environment than girls do came home to me while I was working with a boy who was a disruption in class. Sitting across a table from him, I informed him that he didn't have to yell to be heard. "I'M NOT YELLING," he screamed at me, and I realized he believed he was right. Think about that other group of people that are often louder than everyone else, the elderly. They speak at a level that sounds comfortable to them because they don't hear well. Is it possible that boys' reputation for being loud has the same explanation? Think about the brain lag: boys' brains are developing more slowly than girls' brains, so it stands to reason that the parts of the brain that collect outside stimuli wouldn't be as well developed.

So what does this need for stimuli have to do with reading? We think of reading as a solitary and sedentary activity. Our idealized picture of a child reading would have him curled up under a window on a rainy day, lost in a novel for three hours. That just isn't how many boys read.

For one thing, boys are less likely than girls to sit for extended periods of time to read. Remember why boys and girls read. Girls will tend to read to understand interpersonal relationships. Such relationships take time, and the types of reading girls often do reflect that. The story is likely to turn on long interactions between characters. Relationships require an investment of time, and girls tend to read that way. Boys read to understand actions and consequences, so they are much more likely to read for a short while then get up and do something, maybe even do something inspired by their reading. If they enjoy the experience they may come back and read some more. Amazingly, even when boys and girls read the same amount of time, they do it in different ways. Boys are likely to read in more bursts for shorter periods of time.

> When boys learn words, their brains actually signal the muscles associated with the word, i.e., when a boy learns the word run, the leg muscles are signaled by the brain. Muscle stimulation is part of language attainment for boys. Girls do not learn this way.
> —Louann Brizendine, *The Male Brain*[7]

When boys try to read, especially for long stretches, they often start to fall asleep. Their remedy is to twitch, move, or bounce things off the wall in an attempt to wake up their flagging brains. We may take it as being distracted, lacking focus, or even lacking discipline. Before taking that leap, consider the way many men read.

Personally, I need music or some other noise distraction if I am to read for any amount of time. Music is good, a football game in the background is better, but best of all is a baseball game on the radio. Most baseball games last two and a half to three hours and contain about twenty minutes of real action. I can read away until I hear a cheer, listen to find out who hit a home run, and go back to my book. Men often do any number of things when they read, not just listening to the television, radio, or stereo, but eating breakfast and even driving. That is what audiobooks are, reading that you can do while driving—and men are the heaviest users of audiobooks.

But when a child tries to read with headphones on, or in front of the television, or while kicking a soccer ball against their bedroom wall, or heaven forbid all three, we tell them to be quiet, turn all that stuff off, and concentrate. Sadly, that is exactly what he is trying to do. Obviously the boy doing seven other things while he is reading is overcompensating. He knows on some level that his brain is working sluggishly and that stimuli helps, so he floods his world with stimuli. Instead of overreacting yourself, you can take this knowledge and do a little negotiating. It doesn't take a lot of stimuli to spark the corpus callosum. You can maybe choose the music, preferably not through the headphones pumping directly into his ears, and turn off the television. Even letting him read while crashed out on a couch or floor gives him more physical stimuli than sitting in a hard-backed chair.

That may mean giving up on any carefully designed "homework spaces." Often suggested by teachers, homework spaces are dedicated corners of the home where children can be free of distractions to do their school work and reading. That often means a desk and chair set up facing a blank wall away from all electronic devices and even windows. For someone who needs stimuli to keep their brain humming along, this is torture. Blocking out stimuli is a great strategy for most girls who already have a dominant corpus callosum, and most educators are women, so it is understandable that they would suggest an environment that seems ideal to them. As parents, you need to remember there is a different point of view.

Boys and the ADHD Epidemic

What makes a stimuli-free reading environment at home even more difficult for boys is that they largely spend six or seven hours in a stimuli-free environment at school. School walls are usually bare—at least, until a caring teacher alters them—and painted white or beige. Fluorescent lights in most schools wash out color and emit white noise in the form of a low hum. Windows are usually covered to keep kids from staring out the window when they should be paying attention, despite the fact that refocusing the eyes at height and distance may actually help many boys pay attention. We stuff them in desks designed to keep movement to a minimum.

And the classroom atmosphere is getting worse for boys. No Child Left Behind has made schools spend more time on reading instruction and less time on art, music, gym, recess, and lunch. Boys need the stimuli, play time, and physicality to learn at their best more than the skills-based and repetitive drilling of formal reading instruction. And yet 39 percent of first graders today get less than twenty minutes of recess a day. Seven percent get none.[8]

What is the result of this squeezing of all stimuli from our schools? An explosion of attention deficit/hyperactivity disorder (ADHD), and boys are suffering the most. Researcher Michael Gurian reports that between 80 and 95 percent of hyperactive children in first through third grades are male.[9] Matthew Clavel reported finding six boys diagnosed as ADHD to every girl.[10] In 2003, 14 percent of all boys in America were diagnosed with ADHD by age 16. The number of boys diagnosed with ADHD, birth to age 19, rose 48 percent between 2000 and 2005, the early days of No Child Left Behind.[11] It may be quite some time before we get a clear view of the overall extent of ADHD diagnosis in the first decade of the twenty-first century.

What every parent should remember, especially when informed that your son has ADHD, is that this is a purely symptomatic diagnosis. There is no genetic basis or pathological explanation for the disorder.[12] According to the American Psychiatric Association, "There are no laboratory tests that have been established as diagnostic in the clinical assessment of ADHD."[13] Interestingly, the only biological basis for the disorder seems to be that smaller than average corpus callosa have been observed in ADHD patients.[14] Since most kids with ADHD are male, and males on average have a smaller corpus callosum, this shouldn't surprise us—but it should give us pause.

Diagnosis of ADHD is so varied, it cannot be objective. The three factors that most affect diagnosis rates are gender, race, and socioeconomic status. A joint study by the University of Michigan and University of Texas at Austen published in 2006 found that one in three white boys who live in affluent suburbs are diagnosed with ADHD.[15] Geography matters too. In the Midwest more than 28 percent of all children were diagnosed with ADHD in 2007.[16] That means that if boys make up most diagnoses, then nearly half the boys in the Midwest are officially ADHD!

And just to add to the confusion over ADHD diagnosis, it has been pointed out that childhood depression may mimic ADHD almost perfectly.[17] Now, as a former special needs teacher at a school specializing in ADHD, I am not about to deny that ADHD exists. I have seen cases where children clearly have an imbalance that must be addressed. But the explosion of cases tells me that not all kids who are diagnosed have a real problem, and the unevenness of the diagnosis tells me that it is clearly discriminatory. Boys are being coded for a learning disability based on a natural gender difference and perfectly normal boy behavior. We have defined "being male" as a reading disability.

Honoring How Boys Read

It doesn't take much to make reading an active and engaging experience. For starters, let your son decide how he wants to read. Choice is still the key, and that means if he wants to hang upside down from the front of the couch and read while the basketball game is playing on the television, then that is fine. Don't be too surprised if Dad ends up trying it too.

Understand how frustrating school can be for many boys whose natural tendency to move is quashed for no good reason that he can see, and actually for no good reason. After six or seven hours of that quashing, the last thing he needs to hear is "sit down and do your reading." Trying to force him to read in those circumstances will not only be futile, but it will stress him and you, and convince him that reading is just an extension of the oppressive routine of school. Be willing to allow the option of not reading if that means a better feeling toward reading in the future.

> The Reader's Bill of Rights
> 1. The right not to read.
> 2. The right to skip pages.
> 3. The right to not finish a book.
> 4. The right to reread.
> 5. The right to read anything.
> 6. The right to escapism.
> 7. The right to read anywhere.
> 8. The right to browse.
> 9. The right to read out loud.
> 10. The right to not defend your tastes.
> —Daniel Pennac, *Better Than Life*[18]

When your boy does read, recognize that your picture of reading—maybe including quiet, sedentary, prolonged engagement—may not be what he needs for reading. Allow some stimuli, what you would originally think of as distraction. If he has trouble getting into reading, especially if he talks about it being boring or complains that it makes him sleepy, you can even suggest some stimuli. Some schools are experimenting with using stress balls—squishy balls that can be squeezed repeatedly—to stimulate the brain. They are finding the effect is better listening skills and ease in using language.[19] Have some around the house and take them out whenever your son is feeling twitchy.

> Children's books, on the other hand, can spark a child's imagination. Even heavily illustrated picture books leave some details to the imagination. Each reader will bring her own voice and interpretation to the story—unlike the case with books adapted from television or movies, which simply trigger the child's memory and lack any opportunity for imagination.
> —Jill Bickford, in *Children and Libraries*[20]

For younger boys, have homemade and recycled props for kids to play with after reading books.[21] That does not mean media tie-in toys; those will limit the creativity of play and hence the long-term engagement. Children presented with a toy representing a character they know from television will tend to rigidly rehash the story lines they have observed. A toy or prop without those connections forces the child to create a play environment.[22] Instead, make sure your son's toy area includes clothes, art supplies, and interesting objects that can be used in different ways. With such creative props, children won't act out or draw or paint the story they have read exactly, and that's the point, inventive, rather than imitative play. One reason books not based on television shows are better is because the kids will be less likely to simply play out story lines they see. Books not connected with media are more nuanced and contain more than any television show could, and the imagery exists in the child's head.

Don't crowd your boy. We often think of reading as something that is done in a nook (not the electronic book reader, but a contained place). And while one cliché is the boy reading under the covers with a flashlight, it is just as iconic to see a boy leaning against a tree and reading. Boys think spatially, and sometimes they need more space when they read.[23] Confining him to a chair, a room, or even a house is not honoring the way he reads.

> The lack of boys' success in formal schooling activities . . . can . . . be framed as resistance, both conscious and unconscious, against meaning-less, mindless, boring schooling or workplace activities and assignments.
> —Kathy Sanford, Heather Blair, and Raymond Chodzinski,
> in *Teaching and Learning*[24]

Mostly, think about the reading environment the boy has in school, then do everything you can to make the reading environment at home as different as possible. Do not restrict stimuli by blocking out noise, visually interesting distractions, or the option of moving. And do not under any circumstances get caught checking up on the boy to make sure he is reading. Prying questions that are clearly meant to test or dictated activities, such as "draw me a scene from the book," are transparent attempts to assess, not engage. Boys get enough of that in school, and it is one big reason why so many boys do not read at home.

The Silver Bullet: Reading Aloud

Two researchers at the University of Houston asked thousands of elementary and middle school students what would motivate them to read. The three answers common to both groups were: choice, book ownership, and being read to aloud.[25] A 2001 study asked more than 1,700 sixth graders what made them want to read. Sixty-three percent said free reading time, and 62 percent said being read to aloud by the teacher.[26] Book ownership and free choice and time to read—okay. Most of us could see that. But reading aloud? To middle school kids? Why does this rank so high? There are two reasons: one is practical, and one comes down to . . . you guessed it, stress.

I have from time to time been asked to work with individual boys who are having trouble with reading in school. When I first meet an elementary student this way, I always ask the same question: Do you want to learn how to read? Amazingly, I've never met a boy who has ever been asked that before. We just assume everybody wants to learn how to read. Discouragingly, probably half the boys answer no. When I ask them why not, the most common answer I get is that if they learn to read, then people will stop reading to them. Even worse, they are probably right.

For many boys, especially those who struggle with reading, the last time they enjoyed reading was probably when they were about 3 years old, when reading came down to bedtime reading and story hour at the public library. Being read to brings back those pleasant memories when your only job was to enjoy and, in the case of bedtime reading, be asleep by the end. Within a few years, if the boy fell asleep during reading time, someone would yell at him. How sad is that?

The practical reason is simple: when it comes to learning language, hearing stories read aloud has much the same effect as reading itself.[27] That might be the most revolutionary piece of research about reading ever done. After all, I can't tell you how many times I have heard a teacher tell a parent that their son is reading independently, usually around age 8, so the parent should stop reading to the child. Instead, the child should start reading to the parent. You have to realize that this is punishing your son for learning how to read.

Why does reading aloud improve the listener's reading skills? Everyone knows we learn more vocabulary from reading than we do by memorizing a list of ten vocabulary words a week. We learn words by seeing them used in context, but if you don't read fluently the context is lost. Listening to someone better than you at reading means you get more context, and so you get more vocabulary. You also learn more grammar. How many of us remember all the rules of grammar we were taught in school? No, you know something is not right because "it sounds wrong." Listening to formal language read out loud gives us the background to hear good and bad grammar.

Mostly, listening to books read out loud exposes us to stories and helps us understand how a story is structured, with a beginning, middle, and end. It helps us see how an author can set up an expectation so we expect certain outcomes. It helps us see how arguments are built logically. Knowing how to decode words doesn't equal reading. We need to understand narrative as well, and boys who read less than girls are not exposed to enough narrative to really understand it. Studies done in both England and America confirm that the average teenage boy reads only about 2.3 hours per week.[28] You need to make up a lot of time reading to your son.

Reading aloud to boys is the best answer to how we ignore the brain lag that boys experience all through school. Naturally slower to develop language skills because their brains grow at a different pace than girls, boys are often reading below grade level and are assigned books in school that are too hard for them. They get discouraged, decide they aren't good readers, and stop reading. Parents can blunt the effect by simply reading large chunks of their sons' assigned reading to them. It may feel like cheating, but the research says that your son will gain as much language skill by listening as he would by reading, and a great deal more than if he simply weren't reading.

And that research is pretty open-ended. It doesn't say reading to 6-year-olds is effective, it just says reading aloud helps build reading skills in the listener. As I joke to librarians when training them, you can stop reading to boys when they turn 90 years old and can't hear you anymore. And of course, regardless of the language-building benefits, reading aloud is great for bringing fun back into reading and making reading a shared and supportive activity. If there is one thing you can do to make your son a better reader—and a lifelong reader—read to him and don't stop.

Writing

Can anyone learn to write at all without also knowing how to read?
—Milton Freedman[29]

Milton Freedman's quote is one many writers use to encourage budding writers to read more. When I speak to kids about writing or do writing workshops, I use that sentiment often. The most common question I get is "What advice do you have for someone who wants to be a writer?" The first answer is always: read. But the reverse is true as well. Anyone who wants to grow up to be a reader should write. Reading teaches writers their craft, but writing makes a reader practice his skills in new and productive ways.

In the movie *Dead Poets Society*, Robin Williams is an English teacher at an all-boys school. He gathers his students together and tells them that the main purpose of poetry is to woo women. Joke? Sure, but is there a kernel of truth in there? Jonathan Gottschall points out that some evolutionists see stories as sexual selection. Stories impress girls.[30] At least by their teen years, this may be a powerful motivator to get boys writing.

Okay, that is more than a little tongue-in-cheek, but there are more serious reasons to be concerned about boys and writing as well. The reading gap among twelfth graders may be twice as wide in favor of girls as the math gap is in favor of boys, but the gender gap in writing is six times as wide as the gender gap in math.[31] And writing is nearly as important in this highly verbal world as reading, whether in the workforce or college. English professor Thomas Newkirk puts it bluntly, "Literacy is the currency of college work. Your grading in college is basically based on how well you write."[32]

Our schools were beginning to move powerfully toward highlighting writing in the 1990s and into the new century, with the emergence of writing circles and the writer's workshop. Teachers rode the wave of "differentiated instruction"—teaching to the specific learning styles of individual or small groups of kids—to teach reading in new and innovative ways. They had really just begun to take on the challenge of "differentiated assessment," or allowing kids to show what they had learned in ways as individual as their learning styles. The writer's workshop was the ideal way to demonstrate the language skills needed to be a reader. Then the era of high-stakes, standardized testing set many schools back decades in their writing efforts.

Boys get off to a slow start in writing right out of the blocks. Many boys hate to learn how to write for reasons that have nothing to do with intelligence, brain development, or creativity. They have better gross motor skills, but girls have better fine motor skills. It is almost a running joke that boys' handwriting is atrocious, and they know it. Writing can be downright embarrassing. Manipulation of a writing instrument can be downright painful, and as if all that isn't enough, it makes writing slower for boys than for girls.[33] Research has also proven that poor handwriting affects how teachers see and evaluate boys' writing.[34] Teachers see boys as poor writers early, and boys often internalize that. Once again, stress works against boys and language.

> Most girls write for the teacher. Boys write to entertain each other.
> —Ralph Fletcher, *Boy Writers*[35]

When asked in school how they would like to react to books that are assigned to them, most kids expressed a desire to do so through art projects. The most common answer for how they didn't want to react to books was writing.[36] I think this is probably more so with boys, and I think I know why. Boys generally want their reading to be reinforced, not assessed. It is easier to see a diorama or a picture as an extension of the reading experience. A book report or a summary is just a test to make sure he read the book.

Of course outside of school, there is no need to assess a boy's reading. Yes, you want to make sure he really is reading, but suppress that desire. If you are really curious, ask him what he thought of the book, and use the opportunity to talk about what you are reading. That is sharing, not testing. You want to encourage boys to write not as a response to their reading, but as an extension of it. Boys usually don't want to just observe, they want to imitate. They want to *do* something, and if reading is too passive, writing is the active side of the coin.

Parents can and should encourage their sons to write. Writing exercises language skills, gives boys control over the topics they wish to explore, motivates boys to read more to feed their writing skills, and builds confidence by letting boys work toward their strengths, rather than just being tested on their weaknesses.

There are other kinds of writing, outside of school. The online world of web pages, blogs, e-mail, and instant messaging are in fact writing as well as reading.[37] English professor Jonathan Gottschall points out that we serialize our autobiographies in Twitter and Facebook.[38] Many multiplayer and stand-alone video games create a narrative as players navigate the game, often mirroring the kinds of plots found in fantasy and action-adventure stories. Sports games recreate the kind of drama inherent in any sporting event, and in many sports books.

Many forms of digital writing, such as instant messaging, chat, or texting, are completely impermanent. They are there and gone. That may seem obvious, but the implications are important. With these mediums there is no need—indeed, no real opportunity—to revise and edit. They are strictly utilitarian. If they get the message across, then content means everything and mechanics mean nothing.[39] When boys complain about school writing, these are points they make constantly. In addition, the very impermanence of digital writing allows boys who might need a bit of emotional distance to be more emotionally engaged and expressive.[40] When criticizing boys' school writing, these are concerns adults express just as often.

Boys' Writing Gets No Respect Either

The stereotype of teen writing as angst-ridden poetry and memoirs, despairing lyrics, and just generally deeply personal and dramatic self-reflection is a very incomplete picture.[41] Most of all, it fits almost exclusively the stereotypically female view of reading. Boys' reading gets little respect; boys' writing barely gets noticed, at least until it becomes too violent for adults' taste.

The writer's workshop approach, which rose to prominence by the early 2000s, was a huge step forward in teaching writing. Its success is due largely to the fact that it actually replicates the processes of many successful writers. The whole premise of the writer's workshop is the open topic. Writers must be free to choose what they write about. But the echoes of September 11, Columbine, and the zero-tolerance policies many schools adopted because of them killed that. That final statement, by the way, would get a high school senior suspended in many schools. (Can't used "killed" as a metaphor.)

Post-Columbine, many schools adopted zero-tolerance policies when it comes to violence, and that included students' writing. Any violence in writing could mean a trip to the school counselor.[42] This had the effect of making writing an even more school-bound activity, one that was forced upon kids and that denied the viewpoint of so many boys.

I am not going to argue that boys should write about violence, only that they will, and with some reason. Much like reading violent material, boys write violence as a way to work out their understanding of a foreign idea in a safe environment. Boys don't write violence to be violent; often they do so to understand violence without being violent themselves. In the words of writing expert Ralph Fletcher, "Through written language they can safely grapple with power and danger, issues that make up a big part of a boy's internal world."[43]

Beyond the fear of violent and antisocial topics, boys' choice in school writing is hampered by the standardized testing effect. High-stakes writing tests generally offer a prompt that is generic enough to be used by thousands of students without reference to any shared background knowledge or interest. Such writing has no apparent practical use—few people have jobs where they are required to write about something that they have no special knowledge of—and drains writing of any connection to things that interest the writer. On top of that, the obvious way to prepare for such a test is to do the same thing over and over all year. In schools desperate for time and fearful of the consequences of test failure, this may be the only writing some students do.[44]

Supporting Boys' Writing

Ralph Fletcher, writing advocate and a prominent writer himself, offers this rather blunt assessment in his book *Boy Writers*: "Here's a radical idea: let's bring choice back to the writing classroom. Just let them write. I don't know a better first step to create an environment that will engage our boy writers."[45] I would add that there is little chance that the tide will turn anytime soon in schools, so parents should take any opportunity to support the skill of writing at home.

You can begin to encourage your boy to write by acknowledging the types of writing he already does, whether in social media or video games, or other electronic media, then encouraging him to take the story that already exists and turn it into a piece of writing. A boy who tweets constantly may create the framework of a memoir just by cutting and pasting the various messages about a topic or event. He can even involve friends who can either contribute their own tweets or write a parallel version using their logged messages. Boys can try out any number of variants on a plot by playing a sports or adventure game many times until they get the story line they want.

Find contests for boys to show off their writing. When I moved to the Tulsa area, I quickly entered a creative writing contest run by the Friends of the Tulsa City-County Library. It was a chance for kids, teens, and adults—professionals, hobbyists, and amateurs alike—to compete on a level playing field of short stories, memoirs, and poetry. It was a grand time. During the hourlong presentation of awards, I was the only male to stand on stage. That was a lost opportunity.

Creative writing contests exist at local, state, and even the national level. The incredibly popular author of the Captain Underpants series, Dav Pilkey, had his first book published when he won the Landmark Editions National Written and Illustrated By . . . Awards Contest for Students.[46] Contests add the lure of competition to writing, something that will resonate with many boys.

Expose teens to writers, especially successful young writers.[47] In 2011, I visited a high school in Nebraska and met with the Library Club, a group of students who volunteered at the library, shared their reading, and sometimes acted as a writers' support group. When I asked the twenty or so students how many authors had they met, not a one had met any. Living most of my life in New England where authors are relatively plentiful, I just assumed that most kids were exposed to authors on a regular basis. There were schools that had me in talking to classes every year. That is not always the case. Sadly, too many of our kids think Martians write books and they just fall from the sky. Boys especially, who tend to be experiential learners, will be prone to discount whatever they cannot see. If you want boys to be writers, then boys need to *see* writers.

Bookstores are great places to find authors, and the big chain bookstores in particular are part of a network that regularly sends authors out to the public to promote books. Local libraries also bring in authors. These events are generally free and usually more intimate than you would imagine. Your boy will have a chance to see, meet, even talk with people who write real books. If possible, hammer home the experience by buying a copy of a book that the author can sign.

The Internet and social media provide an opportunity that has never existed to get personal with authors. These days, few authors can afford to be cut off from an audience that expects access, so they have a presence on Facebook, Twitter, or one of the social networking sites catering to readers, such as Goodreads.com. I have an author page there and regularly field questions and comments from readers, who not only get to ask anything they want about my books and the writing process, but can see the books that I read and read my comments about them. "Keep it real" is more than a hip slogan when it comes to boys; it is a necessity, and you can make writing very real to boys when you connect them with real writers.

One activity I use when conducting writing workshops in school can help make writing a game at home or with small groups of boys. It is called "writing yourself out of a corner." It is an exercise that mirrors what real writers do every day when trying to build a believable bridge between different points in a story. The name refers to the tough spot writers get into when they have great ideas that are so funny and wild that they can't make a cohesive story out of them. Because it focuses on plot—an often wild and funny plot—it is appealing to a lot of boys.

To play the game, you need some number of opening lines for a story, and some number of ending lines. The odder and more engaging these lines, the better. You can simply go to a bookstore or library and flip to the first and last pages of numerous books to collect these, or make them up yourself. Here are eight of each that I used at a writer's workshop at an elementary school in Andover, Massachusetts, in 2012:

Opening Lines

1. My little sister wanted a pony for her birthday party.
2. It was the first ever Einstein Elementary School Chess Tournament.
3. I wanted to teach my dog to answer the phone.
4. I was the fastest kid in the fifth grade.
5. I know I should have gotten the brakes fixed on my bike.
6. I just wanted a candy bar from the store.
7. The water didn't look that deep.
8. I forgot to do my math homework.

Closing Lines

1. So the school may not be open for six months.
2. Now none of the toilets at the police station work.
3. My eyebrows are supposed to grow back in a few months.
4. They said I could keep the million dollars.
5. And now I have a pet porcupine.
6. And now my dog has no fur.
7. And the bear got away.
8. And now I have to wash my mom's car every weekend for a month.

Once you have your lists (this or one you come up with on your own) pick a number at random for your opening line and write it at the top of a piece of paper. Then pick another number for your closing line and write that at the bottom of the page. The challenge then is to fill in the actions (plot points) that will connect the two. Everything has to be explained, so having aliens fall from the sky as a plot point only makes things harder. And only actions are allowed. "Susie was sad" is not a plot point, but "Susie cried" is. Once the opening and closing are connected, you can go ahead and write the story.

This is an exercise (call it a game) that a boy can do alone, with a parent, or in a group of boys. If you do it as a group activity—say, as a different activity for a book club you are hosting—then you should all decide on the plot points together, voting if necessary to break up arguments. Then every boy can write their own version of the story. The exercise, especially when done in a group, is loud, active, laugh-inducing, and very much not what happens during most school writing assignments. That, of course, is the appeal.

My goal here is not to tip the world of writing entirely toward boys, but to recognize differences in order to open up the playing field. The approach toward writing taken in many schools may favor girls, but ultimately that is limiting to both boys and girls. If there is richness in reading given that so much variety is out there to be had, how much more so for writing, where the possibilities are endless?

Big Question: Are E-readers the Answer?

Our research indicates that boys who struggle in reading may profit from reading on an e-reader, simply because the act of reading has greater value to them. More value may lead to more engagement, and more engagement may build stronger skills in reading for boys.

—Twyla Miranda et al., in *International Journal of Applied Science and Technology*[48]

Talk about a common question these days: Should I get my son a Kindle? Or a Nook? Or any one of the many electronic readers (e-readers) on the market so he can read electronic books (e-books)? Hidden in the question is the idea that technology will add to the appeal of reading. Twyla Miranda and her colleagues found that to be true in their study in *The International Journal of Applied Science and Technology*. They wrote that "the e-readers appeared to give the reading improvement students some additional confidence. Reading on a technology gadget may have subtly given a message to their peers that 'we too are a part of the 21st technological century.'"[49]

And beyond the cool factor, e-readers may do many of the things we want to do to help boys read. The text-to-audio feature basically turns any electronic text into a read-aloud. Most publishers of high-interest/low-level reading—aimed particularly at struggling readers—keep a close watch on text size, knowing that small text hinders and discourages readers. Electronic reading devices allow you to change the text size at will.

Choice, too, is enhanced by e-readers, because boys can choose their books without worrying about what others think of their reading. A fifth grader who reads at a third-grade level may need to read a second-grade level book to read fluently and easily, but he won't want to be seen reading it. Miranda et al. point out, "Many low-level readers would prefer for their peers to not know the level of books that they are reading, and e-readers could easily house a wide variety of texts on appropriate levels."[50]

And finally, boys are more likely to read on e-readers because that is what they see the men in their lives doing. A survey done by the Pew Research Center's Internet and American Life Project found that "men who own e-reading devices and e-content consumers under age 50 are particularly likely to say they are reading more."[51] Never discount *who* a boy is reading with—a point we will explore further in chapter 5.

NOTES

1. Leonard Sax, *Boys Adrift: The Five Factors Driving the Growing Epidemic of Unmotivated Boys and Underachieving Young Men* (Basic Books, 2007), 24.

2. Carla Hannaford, *Smart Moves: Why Learning Is Not All in Your Head* (Great Ocean Publishers, 1995), 80.

3. Ibid., 81.

4. Michael Gurian and Patricia Henley, with Terry Trueman, *Boys and Girls Learn Differently! A Guide for Teachers and Parents* (Jossey-Bass, 2001), 30.

5. Leonard Sax, *Why Gender Matters: What Parents and Teachers Need to Know about the Emerging Science of Sex Differences* (Doubleday, 2005), 23.

6. Sax, *Boys Adrift*, 118.

7. Louann Brizendine, *The Male Brain* (Broadway Books, 2010), 26.

8. Peg Tyre, *The Trouble with Boys: A Surprising Report Card on Our Sons, Their Problems at School, and What Parents and Educators Must Do* (Crown Publishers, 2008), 101.

9. Gurian and Henley, *Boys and Girls Learn Differently*, 36.

10. Matthew Clavel, "Save the Males: A Case for Making Schools Friendlier to Boys," *American Enterprise*, July/August 2005, 30.

11. Tyre, *The Trouble with Boys*, 111.

12. Hannaford, *Smart Moves*, 198.

13. Aaron Kipnis, *Angry Young Men: How Parents, Teachers, and Counselors Can Help "Bad Boys" Become Good Men* (Jossey-Bass, 2002), 63.

14. Hannaford, *Smart Moves*, 80.

15. Sax, *Boys Adrift*, 34–35.

16. Helen Schneider, "My Child and ADHD: Chances of Being Diagnosed," *Pediatrics for Parents*, September 2007, 9.

17. Sax, *Boys Adrift*, 198.

18. Daniel Pennac, *Better Than Life* (Coach House Press, 1994), 170–71.

19. Gurian and Henley, *Boys and Girls Learn Differently*, 177 and 226.

20. Jill Bickford, "Consumerism: How It Impacts Play and Its Presence in Library Collections," *Children and Libraries*, Winter 2010, 56.

21. Nancy Carlsson-Paige and Diane E. Levin, *Who's Calling the Shots? How to Respond Effectively to Children's Fascination with War Play, War Toys and Violent TV* (New Society Publishers, 1990), 105.

22. Bickford, "Consumerism," 53.

23. Gurian and Henley, *Boys and Girls Learn Differently*, 47.

24. Kathy Sanford, Heather Blair, and Raymond Chodzinski, "A Conversation about Boys and Literacy," *Teaching and Learning*, Spring 2007, 9.

25. Teri S. Lesesne, *Naked Reading: Uncovering What Tweens Need to Become Lifelong Readers* (Stenhouse, 2006), 37.

26. Catherine Sheldrick Ross, Lynne (E. F.) McKechnie, and Paulette M. Rothbauer, *Reading Matters: What the Research Reveals about Reading, Libraries, and Community* (Libraries Unlimited, 2006), 66.

27. Stephen D. Krashen, *The Power of Reading: Insights from the Research*, 2nd ed. (Libraries Unlimited, 2004), 77–81.

28. English study: Adi Bloom, "Girls Go for Little Women but Boys Prefer Lara," *Times Educational Supplement*, March 15, 2002, 18; American study: Steven J. Ingles et al., *A Profile of the American Sophomore in 2002: Initial Results from the Base Year of the Education Longitudinal Study of 2002* (National Center for Education Statistics, 2005), 75.

29. Richard Whitmire, *Why Boys Fail: Saving Our Sons from an Educational System That's Leaving Them Behind* (American Management Association, 2010), 68.

30. Jonathan Gottschall, *The Storytelling Animal: How Stories Make Us Human* (Houghton Mifflin, 2012), 27.

31. Jeffrey D. Wilhelm and Michael Smith, *Reading Don't Fix No Chevys: Literacy in the Lives of Young Men* (Heinemann, 2002), 1.

32. Whitmire, *Why Boys Fail*, 28–29.

33. Ralph Fletcher, *Boy Writers: Reclaiming Their Voices* (Stenhouse, 2006), 73.

34. Whitmire, *Why Boys Fail*, 69.

35. Fletcher, *Boy Writers*, 113.

36. Lesesne, *Naked Reading*, 44–47.

37. Ross, McKechnie, and Rothbauer, *Reading Matters*, 3.

38. Gottschall, *The Storytelling Animal*, 18.

39. Fletcher, *Boy Writers*, 43.

40. Ibid., 34–36.

41. Ross, McKechnie, and Rothbauer, *Reading Matters*, 123.

42. Whitmire, *Why Boys Fail*, 70.

43. Fletcher, *Boy Writers*, 54.

44. Ibid., 44.

45. Ibid., 45.

46. "The Almost Completely True Adventures of Dav Pilkey," www.pilkey.com, accessed August 28, 2012.

47. Ross, McKechnie, and Rothbauer, *Reading Matters*, 126.

48. Twyla Miranda et al., "Reluctant Readers in Middle School: Successful Engagement with Text Using the E-reader." *International Journal of Applied Science and Technology*, November 2011, 89.

49. Ibid.

50. Ibid.

51. Lee Rainie et al., *The Rise of E-reading* (Pew Research Center's Internet and American Life Project, 2012), 4.

What Boys Read

Big Question: Should Boys Read Girl Books?

Shortly after the publication of my first book, *Escapade Johnson and Mayhem at Mount Moosilauke*, I received the following e-mail:

Dear Mike,

I am a grandmother, and love to buy books for my nine year old grandson. I saw your article in the Portsmouth Herald about your books. I immediately went to Barnes and Noble in Portsmouth to check them out. I always read the entire book to see if it is proper for my grandson, without cursing, improper behavior, etc., before I give it to my grandson.

I took it home and read the book. On the whole, it is a wonderful book. A fun story, with a lot of adventure. I liked how you juxtaposed the wealthy children with the middle class children, *[which has to be the first and only Marxist interpretation of my writing]* but there are 8 pages that I find inappropriate for my grandson.

[Then she goes on to list them, with page numbers, things such as:]

- The boys throwing spitballs at the teacher every day.
- Substitute teachers being locked in the boiler room, filling hairnets with bugs before the cafeteria ladies could put them on, and second graders chased up trees with enormous dogs.
- Leaping on a desk, falling off hitting his head on the tile floor.
- Removing screws from teacher's chair, bringing pet cockroaches to school, and Cherilyn and Katrina gluing Davy's pants to chair.
- Pulling the boys pants down around his ankles.

[And my personal favorite:]

- Scat was fine, poop wasn't necessary.

[Which, by the way, will be the title of my autobiography, should I be fortunate enough to write one, or alternatively, the epithet on my tombstone.]

I really do like the story a lot. It is the perfect type of adventure boys would love to read, but it can be just as much fun and exciting without the above mention.

Sincerely, Fran

The author of this letter was just wrong. The story would not have been nearly as fun or exciting without these things. Mostly it shows a lack of understanding of, and respect for, the literature that appeals to boys. Children, of course, are all unique, so generalizations are flawed, but there are general trends that describe large groups of people, if not everyone. There are aspects of literature that appeal to large numbers of boys. Most important, for many reluctant boy readers, these trends seem to be magnified.

Let's be clear about one thing up front: most boys read, even those that you never see reading and those who would deny it to their dying day. Boys read baseball cards, the box scores in the newspaper, magazines, the directions to their video games, web pages full of "cheat codes" for their video games, and cereal boxes. Boys read things that teachers overlook, such as "digital literacy," or text that exists online.[1] Many boys may not read books—at least, not the books we want them to read—but they read. They often don't think adults will count their reading as "real" reading, and they may be right, so they often don't share their reading with us.

Magazines offer familiar and predictable formats, layouts, and subjects.[2] Parents sometimes despair that their boys' reading is so narrow when he reads the latest skateboard magazine every month, while not reading much else. It is the narrowness that appeals to the boy, for the same reason that so many boys read only familiar series. It is a stress reaction; boys often feel unsure of their abilities and distrustful of reading, so they concentrate on reading things they know they can handle and will enjoy.

Another reason that boys read newspapers and magazines is because that is what they see dads read. A 1996 study asked kids which parent reads more books, and they answered mothers ten times more often than fathers. Which parent read more newspapers? The children answered fathers ten times more often than mothers.[3] A more recent survey shows men reading fewer magazines and reading more online, including online magazines. "Men aren't migrating so much from the content of magazines as from the format."[4] If boys are imitating fathers' reading, this is a trend every parent of a boy should keep an eye on.

We may want boys' reading books, but it is dangerous to discount all these other ways that boys read. It gives the impression that what boys like to read isn't "real" reading, and that is what creates boys who hide their reading, and boys that identify themselves as nonreaders before reading can become a habit. Researcher Michael Smith asked high school freshmen boys how much they read, and over half the boys answered not at all. Those are 14-year-old boys identifying themselves as nonreaders.[5] And that perception is hard to break. In 1998, UCLA asked their incoming freshmen on the first day of classes how many hours they spend reading for pleasure. Thirty-five percent—more than a third of the young men—told their college that they did not read for pleasure.[6]

The Young Adult Library Services Association (YALSA), the group that represents librarians who work with teenagers, conducted a survey in 2001 that asked teens who identified themselves as nonreaders why they didn't read. The number one answer wasn't that they were too busy, that it was too hard, or that it wasn't cool. The teens didn't read because it was boring.[7] That tells me we aren't giving teens books that engage them, and if most nonreaders are boys it may come down to what we consider an engaging book for boys.

He HATES That Book

A colleague of mine, a public librarian, was called in for a conference by her sixth-grade son's teacher. Jeremy (not his real name) was your typical 11-year-old boy: active, mischievous, and not one of the great English scholars of his generation. He started sixth-grade English so well, though, that his teacher was astounded. He aced every test, completed every homework assignment, and leapt energetically into class discussions. Then, a few weeks into the school year, everything changed. Suddenly he was back to his old ways, not doing homework, zoning out in class, failing every test miserably. It was time for the teacher to have a sit down with Mom.

The teacher laid out the problem as she saw it: Jeremy had lost focus, gotten lazy. He could do the work; that much was clear from his early performance. The mother pointed out that Jeremy had loved the first book the class had read, which was *Maniac Magee* by Jerry Spinelli (Little, Brown Young Readers, 1999). Jeremy had actually done his homework twice most nights, reading the assigned passage then going back to find the funny parts. He would follow his mother around the kitchen, reading aloud to her while she prepared dinner.

But when that book was done, Jeremy could not stomach the second book, *Julie of the Wolves* by Jean Craighead George (HarperTeen, 2003). Not only did he not enjoy the book, but it addressed things about girls that he, a sixth-grade boy, simply did not want to know. He went so far as to try negotiating for extra chores if he would be allowed to skip his reading. The mother said to the teacher, "You have to understand, he really hates this book."

The teacher replied, "I know, the boys always do."

This sixth-grade teacher not only dismissed half of her class with a phrase, but dismissed half of every class for every year that she assigned this book. The question must be asked, if she knows half her class will despise a book, why does she keep assigning it? The answer lies in how we think about kids and reading, and especially how we look at the books that appeal to boys as opposed to those that appeal to girls.

Ironically, if Jeremy had simply not responded to a book that appealed to him, he may never have come to his teacher's attention and could have avoided having his mother called in for a teacher conference. So often, we simply think of boys as nonreaders until we are proved wrong. If we look at results, we have good reason to do so.

Before We Get Too Specific

I've long felt that the teaching of classic literature to school children is a huge mistake. The vast majority of kids do not appreciate it, do not like it, and too many end up hating reading as a result. Schools should look at the encouragement of reading as an actual goal, and design a curriculum around that. Get kids to learn that reading can be fun and they will learn a lot more in life than they ever will by studying Shakespeare or discussing the life of Holden Caulfield.

—Bill Teschek, public librarian

We have to be very careful when trying to understand the kinds of books boys like to read. It is easy to fall into the trap of equating "reading" with very specific fiction books known as "literary fiction." The 2004 study *Reading at Risk*, published by the National Endowment for the Arts, caused a huge amount of hand-wringing about how reading was a dying art. There may be some truth in the study, but it is worth noting that the "reading" they are talking about doesn't include nonfiction.[8] Other studies and commentaries exclude genre fiction (i.e., science fiction, fantasy, gothic, humor), and precious few consider online reading or comic books.

Our literature for children includes both fiction and nonfiction, and fiction means both the novels that kids are more likely to run into in their school reading and various genres, which get little to no attention in English classes. Boys favor the genres over novels, because novels are inherently character-based and the genres tend to focus more on plot.

Boys' reading will often be short; no surprise there. Boys are more likely than girls to be reading below grade level, so if they have to read a book at grade level, they are going to try to minimize the pain. Plus, shorter books will seem to be less of a chore. Many boys will be drawn to series books, again to limit the struggles associated with reading. The hardest ten pages of any book are the first ten pages. That is when the reader must become accustomed to the writing style, setting, dialect, and a hundred other factors. In a series, the boy will go through that process only once and can then enjoy the rest of the series.

Also, for boys who find little reading of interest to them, series give them the prospect of always having the next book in mind when they do find something they like. Series also help build empathy—something many parents worry about when they see the impersonal nature of so much of boys' reading—by extending the contact with certain characters. Unfortunately, series tend to get little respect. One commentator in *Booklist* noted, "In the family of children's literature, fiction series books are often considered distant stepchildren, that is, if they are considered at all."[9]

> Most people think of fiction as a wildly creative art form. But this just shows how much creativity is possible inside a prison. Almost all story makers work within the tight confines of problem structure, whether knowingly or not.
> —Jonathan Gottschall, *The Storytelling Animal*[10]

For similar reasons, many boys will be devoted to reading in a single genre. Boys that have had bad experiences with reading, and who are fearful that the next book thrust upon them will be as dull as the last, may seek out familiar ground. Many parents bemoan the boy who only reads (fill in the blank). We will meet one such parent in the next few pages. But why the discomfort over narrow reading?

Here it is the stress of the parent that is in play. We are so worried about the development of our kids as readers that we forget they are displaying the same types of behaviors that we excuse in ourselves. There is ample evidence that adults who choose books based on a specific genre or author are far more likely to like and finish those books than when they browse.[11]

Does boys' reading seem formulaic to you? It is often a charge, but as English professor Jonathan Gottschall points out, almost all fiction is formulaic. Writers could write books in all kinds of ways—consider James Joyce's *Finnegan's Wake*—but only a very narrow structure is very satisfying.[12] When people complain that boys' reading, or romance fiction, or horse club books are formulaic, they mean that they don't like what the authors in these genres do with the formula. If you want boys to read, finish, and enjoy books, don't balk at the narrowness of their reading.

> Edgy subject matter may feel like it's sending a confused or conflicting message, but the content is out there. The scariest fiction allows teens a vicarious experience, a forewarning from a safe zone, and anyone familiar with inner-city street life will attest that the real side of scary can be fatal. Having youth read "all about it" is preferable to living some of it.
> —Allison Follos, school librarian, *Reviving Reading*[13]

Remember that boys will often be attracted to edgy books. Psychologically, they need to explore the edges of their experience. Bruce Coville "maintains that little 'appropriate' literature for young boys was written prior to his books. His observation is that young boys are by nature mischievous and they want to read about male characters who do 'naughty' not nasty things."[14] Is it hard to understand the appeal of the naughty? You are not supposed to understand it, because you are not the target audience. You are not a 12-year-old boy.

What follows is a look at the types of books that many boys will enjoy, what I call *boys' literature*. That is not to say that all boys will like these types of books, that all boys *should* like these types of books, or that girls won't like these types of books. This is just a look at the types of books that appeal to a lot of boys so you can understand what they are, why boys like them, and maybe when to offer them to a boy who is resistant to reading or just looking for something new.

Always remember that what boys need most is choices in their reading, and ultimately control of their own reading. The researcher William Brozo found that "choice and control are two ingredients commonly missing in instruction provided to adolescent boys who are not reading as would be expected for their grade level and who are disinterested and reluctant readers."[15] So use these suggestions to put more books in front of your boy, then support whatever it is he chooses to read. Look to the lists at the end of this book for recent titles of books that fit these descriptions.

Nonfiction

> What turned my son off from reading? He read a lot of nonfiction and books with science and technology facts. He was never much into fiction, but read a little: Spiderwick, Harry Potter. Then, in fifth grade, he got a teacher who used fiction to teach other subjects like social studies. And she seemed to pick the most boring books. They may have had the content she was looking for, but the books themselves were tedious. As for me, I got turned off of fiction in high school, when I got into honors English classes and had to read Crime and Punishment and Anna Karenina, etc. I thought if this is fiction, I'm having none of it.
>
> —Jacqueline Jaeger Houtman, mother and author of *The Reinvention of Edison Thomas*

When we talk about the types of reading that have boy appeal, we first and foremost need to speak of nonfiction. Teachers, librarians, and parents often see a boy with a nonfiction book in hand and respond with, "That's fine, now get a book you can read." Boys often see nonfiction not as a vehicle for finding specific information, but as a way to better understand the world around them, of acquiring the rules and tools they so desire. In short, they read nonfiction the way we expect children to read fiction. Adult men often see nonfiction the same way. An all-men's reading club in Roanoke, Virginia, celebrated for its vibrancy and lasting-power, chooses nonfiction for half of their books.[16]

> That book is annoying. It provided absolutely no information on how to kill mockingbirds.
>
> —Eric Moreau, a teenage chess student of mine

Dr. Ray Doiron of the University of Prince Edward Island observed ten thousand free reading choices made by children in grades 1–6 from their classroom libraries. Boys in his study chose three nonfiction books for every four fiction books. That finding, in and of itself, should tell us how important nonfiction is in the life of the boy reader. In addition, Doiron looked at the books in the class-room libraries involved and found that more than 85 percent of the books were fiction.[17] Boys, when given free range, found almost half their reading in non-fiction, despite the fact there was virtually no nonfiction to choose from. This study should also caution us; the fact that these classroom libraries were more than 85 percent fiction tells us how easy it is for us adults to underestimate the value of nonfiction.

Many nonfiction books give boys back the illustrations we took out of their fiction books when they were 8 years old. Pictures can be a powerful stimulant to a boy's brain, and they help children read at a higher level by giving visual clues to aid in comprehension.[18] Boys rely more on these clues than girls do, partly because such clues stimulate the right side of the brain, which tends to be better developed in boys.[19] If boys feel stressed about not reading at a higher level, then illustrations can help them succeed and feel successful.

Nonfiction is such a broad category of books that it is worth mentioning some more specific types. Not all nonfiction is created equal. After all, we wouldn't think of knitting books as having broad boy appeal. (Though remember, some boys will happily jump into all sorts of needlecrafts, which are practical and physical, and produce a real product.) Narrative nonfiction, the kind of books that tell a story, tends to have more boy appeal. Look at how popular history and biography are among adult men. You can usually look for books written by journalists, who understand better than most writers how to tell a story and do it quickly and efficiently. Books such as Ken Silverstein's *The Radioactive Boy Scout: The True Story of a Boy and His Backyard Nuclear Reactor* (Random House, 2004) and James L. Swanson's *Chasing Lincoln's Killer* (Scholastic, 2009) are great examples of narrative nonfiction written in a journalistic style.

> Of his own volition, when he was about two or three years old, he chose a book off the "Bargains" shelf at a Borders . . . It is called "Dangerous Animals" and is part of a "Little Guides" collection put out by Fog City Press. I remember being amused by this choice, but this is another book that is still on his shelf (it is quite tattered at this point) and was a die-hard favorite . . . It is a small book, about 4″ x 6″, but over 300 pages long, divided into chapters with titles like "Tusks, Horns, and Antlers" and "Venomous Creatures of the Land." He was already very interested in all forms of animal life, and this just added to the fascination.
>
> —Tara Tuller Dadd, mother

On the other end of the spectrum, encyclopedic nonfiction often has a great deal of boy appeal. Books with tons of little, high interest facts that can be nibbled on feed the way boys often read for little bits of time. It is reading as grazing. *Guinness World Records*, published annually, and *Ripley's Believe It or Not* (Ripley's, 2012) are perennial favorites. Joy Masoff's *Oh Yuck! The Encyclopedia of Everything Nasty* (Workman, 2000) and *Oh Yikes! History's Grossest, Wackiest Moments* (Workman, 2000) are other great examples.

Boys are often attracted to coded language; to riddles, puzzles, word games, and the like. Such reading is short and challenging to the mind, and often requires more thinking than actual reading. In addition, it turns language into a game. It also levels the playing field for many boys who struggle with language. Boys may not understand coded language, but neither does anyone else. For once, boys are on an even footing with the world around them. Yes, it is still a stress issue.

Some people worry that if boys read primarily nonfiction, they will miss out on the social clues that fiction readers gain from their books. There is some truth to this argument. Psychologists Keith Oatley and Raymond Mar found that "people who consume a lot of fiction outperformed heavy nonfiction readers on tests of social ability."[20] There is a reason that girls—more likely to see the world through social eyes—are also more likely to prefer fiction. But before you get too scared, remember that the study tests fiction readers against nonfiction readers. How would the nonfiction readers do against nonreaders? Reading nonfiction, especially narrative nonfiction, is likely to enhance social skills to some extent, even if not as much as fiction.

Finding suggestions for nonfiction books can be harder than finding lists of great fiction books. The National Council of Teachers of English offers the Orbis Pictus Award for Outstanding Nonfiction for Children (www.ncte.org/awards/orbispictus). The Association for Library Service to Children (ALSC), a division of the American Library Association, presents the Robert F. Sibert Informational Book Medal (www.ala.org/alsc/awardsgrants/bookmedia/sibertmedal). And of course there will be lists of great nonfiction titles especially for boys at the end of this book.

Realistic Fiction: Humor, Action-Adventure, Historical Fiction, Mysteries, and Sports

Humor has long been a way to reach boys with reading. Why? Stress is always an issue when it comes to reluctant or resistant readers. Many boys understand that they do not read up to grade level or as well as their classmates. Then they have to face the concern, or consternation, of adults who worry about their lack of reading. Humor is a great release for boys, especially if it is edgy humor that flies in the face of the adults who are pressuring them. The fact that adults often despise their choice of reading materials only adds to its appeal.

Adults may sometimes enjoy humor for kids, but it is always suspect and we tend to shy away from offering it to children unless it is squeaky-clean—and you can spell that b-o-r-i-n-g. Jon Scieszka, the great boy humorist, is quoted as saying, "I can't think of a funny book that my kids ever had to read in school."[21] When Wilhelm and Smith surveyed 49 boys about their connection to reading, "none of our boys could remember reading anything they thought was funny in school."[22]

Robert Fulghum, well known as a writer of wise and wry humor for adults, wrote in the last chapter of his book *It Was on Fire When I Lay Down on It* that after writing that book he actually considered going back and taking out all the funny parts. He noted, "Humor is a bit suspect—conventional wisdom says it takes away from serious writing."[23] If even the author of *All I Really Need to Know I Learned in Kindergarten* (Villard, 1988) must be uncomfortable about humor, how do we expect boys to respect it?

Boys are active creatures, and they will seek to connect their reading to what they like, so action-based stories about sports and the great outdoors will always be big draws for boys. They will want to read about characters doing what they enjoy, and think they would enjoy, doing. Sports and action-adventure stories tend to be plot-driven, not character-driven.

> I had an 8th grader last year who came to me basically aliterate. Standardized tests showed that he could read, but he told me he'd only read about war and fighting, so I started him off with Hunger Games. After he got through that series, I just made sure to have a constant stream of books with something to do with war in them. Over the school year, he read the Ender's Game series, Long Way Gone, and any other historical novels involving war he could get his hands on. At the end of the year, he was reading popular history books and memoirs about soldiers on his own.
> —Katherine Landau Wright, teacher

Mysteries and historical fiction are very broad categories that cause a great deal of confusion. Each is so broad that it easily covers very boy-friendly books as well as some that are really not what the typical boy is looking for. The dividing line is basically plot. Is the book about a series of actions leading to a resolution? Or is it about characters reflecting and changing? Of course most books have both, but it comes down to where the focus is. It is no surprise that war stories are among the most popular historical fiction books among boys; war is often a powerful plot mover.

Mysteries have a long tradition of appealing to boys and men; just think about Sherlock Holmes and Robert Parker's Spencer books. But then there is also Nancy Drew and Elizabeth George. Be careful about pushing a book just because it is a mystery and ask yourself if it is more about the detective or the detecting. Better yet, ask your son.

Much of historical fiction can be seen divided into two types. First, there are the books where the historical setting is integral to the story; the where and when help build an exciting world that is new and different to the reader. These are the boy-friendly books. Others use the historical setting as an interesting backdrop to set the characters against. These are less boy-friendly. Always remember, though, that seeing a boy who likes history and giving him historical fiction may backfire. Why would he want to read something made up when he likes reading the real thing? Sometimes it is our own prejudices against nonfiction that make us try to translate history to historical fiction.

Fantastical Fiction: Fantasy, Science Fiction, Gothic, and Magical Realism

> My proudest achievement as a librarian is hooking one particular boy on reading. He would only come in for movies (while his sister carried books out by the armful) and turned his nose up at every book suggestion. Eventually, after coming in for movies—and to play video games on our Game Days—we wore him down! I believe The Last Apprentice was his first series, and then we was off! Now he complains he's read just about everything in my JF (Juvenile Fiction) and YA (Young Adult) section, and he makes suggestions for books for me to buy.
>
> —Scott Campbell, public librarian

If there is one genre that can turn a nonreader into a voracious reader, it is fantasy. Like the books mentioned above, and the great fantasy series The Last Apprentice by Joseph Delaney, fantastical fiction offers those reluctant readers great plot lines, long series, and real adventure. Unfortunately, that is often not enough for adults who are so stressed about boys' reading that they fail to see the great gift they have been given.

A friend of mine once called me over to discuss the reading habits of his son, who he said was in serious trouble. Dad led me to his son's room and showed me a bookcase filled with paperback series fantasy. Dad explained that the son would read through the entire bookcase every couple of months, then go back and read it all again. The father told me that he needed to get his son away from fantasy or he would never become a reader. Never become a reader? The son read more than his father and me combined!

Adults often see fantasy as a stepping stone to more serious, "real" reading. Science fiction tends to get even less respect. One researcher reported that her son told her, "Some teachers treated sci-fi books like they were pornography."[24] And gothic horror? Many adults treat it as radioactive, at least until it morphs into "gothic romance" with shiny vampires and teen girls writing endlessly in their diaries about their angsty feelings.

Why this indifference, and even hostility? Educators tend to value introspection in reading. We want children exploring their feelings, so we want our characters spending more time reflecting than doing something. A noble goal, sure, and educators may be excused for trying to make reading into a lesson plan, but that is more in line with the way girls read. Girls tend to look inward to understand their world. Boys tend to look outward, placing themselves in a larger world that they can change by acting. If a book isn't inward-looking, we tend to dismiss it as simple escapism.

Girls, it is commonly noted, are more drawn to realistic fiction, but many adults forget how much many adults value escapist literature. Also, fantasy may be much more than escapism for boys, giving them the freedom to explore very real issues with an emotional distance, or comfort zone.[25] In a study of boys choosing books on their own at a large bookstore, the researcher noted, "For all of the boys, the escapist qualities of imaginative fiction were strongly preferred over the immediate connections to their lives that young adult realistic fiction might provide."[26]

Science fiction and fantasy have great appeal to many boys because the books' basic structure is so active. These are plot-based stories. What people do matters, but that doesn't mean characters don't develop. Frodo Baggins learns a great deal about himself during the course of The Lord of the Rings series, but his introspection clearly isn't the point of the books. I would defy anyone to read Ender's Game, Orson Scott Card's science fiction classic, and tell me it doesn't say a great deal about the human experience. But the book is about intergalactic war.

These forms begin with the concept of an individual discovering a new world and journeying out to find a place in that world. For those who don't read these genres, science fiction is basically about a world that could be; fantasy is about a world that does not exist. Gothic horror is a subgenre of fantasy that is sometimes hard to distinguish. Here is the shorthand version: fantasy is all about the battle of good against evil from the perspective of good. Gothic horror looks at the battle of good against evil while looking over the shoulder of evil. That perspective is what makes it so hard for many parents to accept.

And let's face it, these fantastical genres are plot-driven, meaning lots of action that will usually slip into violence. In this post-Columbine era, even the discussion of violence around children is tough to deal with. But remember why boys read, to explore the parts of the world they do not understand. Gothic's dark nature appeals to many boys because it is the dark corners of the world that are most mysterious. And remember, it is easier for boys to explore these dark topics at arm's length. We may wonder why boys need to make up scary creatures when they live in a world filled with plenty of real monsters, but that is exactly why they need a safe, fantastical world to meet evil head-on.

Visual Fiction: Comics, Manga, and Graphic Literature

If nonfiction is popular with boys partly because it gives boys back their illustrations, of course boys will be drawn to books that rely heavily on illustrations. Comic books probably saved a generation of boy readers, and still get no respect. They should. Visual clues help a reader understand the story, even if the language is a bit above him. That means boys can read at a higher level if the book is heavily illustrated. Boys rely more on illustrations than girls do, partly because they stimulate the right side of the brain, and added stimuli is one thing that helps wake up a boy's brain and make it better able to handle language.[27]

Today, boys have the book-length stories told in comic book fashion, known by teachers and librarians as *graphic novels*. The term is unfortunate; comics of course are just a format. The content can be anything. Many of these books are nonfiction and most of the fiction falls into one or more of the genres, most commonly fantasy, so they are not novels at all. Perhaps *visual literature* is a better term, or *sequential art*. Whatever you call these books, they deserve some attention if you want to reach boys. "Comics" were called that originally because they were, first and foremost, funny, so there is a strong tradition of humor in these books. Even more popular today is *manga*, a Japanese format of comic books that looks like a bulky magazine. Manga tends to come in long series, so there is always a next book.

Too often parents, teachers, and librarians automatically look down on any book with pictures. The rise of graphic novels and manga is helping to reverse this trend, but these are often viewed as a stepping stone, as having value only if they lead to "real" reading later on. If you think this way, try to change your way of thinking. There is nothing inherent in illustrated works that makes them any less reading, just as nonfiction is not a lesser form of reading than fiction. If you can't change your thinking, don't let your son hear you talk this way. He will come to believe, as they have with comic books, that these formats do not constitute "real" reading.

Christian Fiction

Like visual literature, Christian fiction is not a genre. It is a specific sensibility that underpins the work. Its appeal is based on the presence of a specific religious worldview among the characters and the absence of the rough language and situations that are common in modern literature. This makes for a very nonspecific definition, and people will disagree as to what belongs and what doesn't.

Giles Gunn helpfully pointed out three ways religion can be presented in fiction. It can be *"complementary,"* meaning the book assumes the place of religion is central to life and works within that comfortable framework. *"Oppositional"* literature keeps religion as the focus, but deals with challenges to faith and the exploring of faith, though in most cases faith is affirmed in the end. The *"alternative"* approach deals with what would be considered religious themes or ideals, but outside the realm of religion.[28] Everyone would consider complementary works to be Christian fiction; few if any would consider alternative works to be so. It's the middle category that raises questions. Some Christian readers do not want to read about questioning faith; others want exactly that. Boys, being often exploratory readers and drawn to the tension of conflict, are more likely to be drawn to this approach.

> [T]he core readership for Christian fiction didn't want speculative fiction. They wanted bonnets and buggies, not mutant alien vampires who will eat your brains . . . If it weren't for that pesky C. S. Lewis, they'd be able to say that all magic in Christian fiction is of the devil. Narnia notwithstanding, they still shy away from anything fantastical.
> —Jeff Gerke, Christian publisher[29]

While Christian novels certainly existed since there were novels, the explosion in Christian publishing really began in the mid-1970s.[30] From the start, Christian fiction books—and especially those for kids and teens—were mostly historical fiction, often romance; and most critics admit the target audience was mostly female.[31] Then there came a rush of realistic fiction, mostly teen issue books. Frank Peretti and others like him added a new twist with gothic-style thrillers, making more edgy-type books acceptable to Christian readers by framing conflicts as spiritual battles.[32]

More recently, there have been books in a wide range of genres based on a Christian sensibility—good news for boys who might not have been inspired by the earlier fare. Now there are Christian books with edgy themes, exciting plots, and real suspense. Even fantasy has found its place. Allen Arnold, a publisher at the prominent Christian publishing house Thomas Nelson, noted that "the stories of the fantastic and supernatural actually make more sense within the context of Christian fiction. These stories involve angels, demons, and the unseen but eternal reality that surrounds us."[33]

> At the very least, a story of children orphaned by the Rapture would tap into every child's abandonment fears . . . It is undeniable that young people will be attracted to the techno-thriller, fast-paced narrative of *Left Behind: The Kids*, but it is equally true that the focus on the earth's destruction and the annihilation of the enemies of Christ can . . . terrify many of them who will fixate on the impending doom.
> —Anita Gandolfo, *Faith and Fiction*[34]

If many parents are uncomfortable with the edginess of boys' literature, then it can't be surprising that many parents who want a Christian perspective to underlie some or all of their sons' reading would be even more uncomfortable. Forget about the mainstream press, ostensibly Christian books can be edgy too. A librarian at a Catholic school once pointed out that she understood the boy appeal of many of the books I was promoting, but there was no way she could put most of it in her school library. My point to her, and to all parents who worry about their sons' reading inclinations, is that it is not the particular edginess that matters to most boys, but the fact that it is edgy.

A book doesn't need harsh language, graphic violence, or sexual undertones to be boy-friendly. Sometimes it just needs tension. Conflict over religious principles is still conflict. The challenge of living out one's ideals against a dominant society that does not share them is a heroic story, just like the challenge of competing at the highest level of sports. Christian fiction can be boy-friendly, and parents don't have to share the attraction to see why it appeals. One of the book lists at the end of this book gives a few examples of Christian fiction books with boy appeal. Don't expect them all to be "gentle reads," so be involved with your boy's reading, but try to remember that it is both Christian and boy reading.

But What about Poetry?

> To some men, more comfortable with the literal and the explicit, it seems
> that both poems and women expect you to read between the lines. What
> teachers see as subtlety or implication sometimes gets translated in boys'
> minds into a blind hunt for secret messages and the perverse notion that
> literature has hidden meanings. What kind of nutty person would try to
> hide meaning? Why can't they just come out and tell you what they mean?
> —B. Pirie, *Teenage Boys and High School English*[35]

And then there is poetry. Remember that poetry is simply a form, or in reality an
almost endless series of forms. What matters most is the content. Many parents
see a boy that loved Bill Peet's funny poetry picture books and are excited to
give him more poetry as he gets older. In many cases, it was the funny, not the
poetry, that the boy loved. Especially for boys who are struggling or reluctant
readers, poetry that hides meaning in flowery language or heavy symbolism is
just adding work and delaying the payoff. We want boys to enjoy poetry because
it is such a powerful use of language. I understand; I am a poet myself. But the
form itself doesn't have appeal to a lot of boys, and pushing them to read it
when they aren't ready is just likely to convince them they don't like it.

No More Dead Dogs

> A possible implication of these results is that children don't know what
> is best for them; another is that Newbery and Caldecott judges have
> different standards than the real audience of children's and adolescent
> literature.
> —Joanne Ujiie and Stephen Krashen, in *Knowledge Quest*[36]

Be careful about pushing too hard to get boys to read the "best" or "great"
books. We all want kids to experience wonderful books because that is what
will inspire them to become readers. One measure of greatness is the John
Newbery Medal, given every year to the best book for children. But whenever
a book is marked as great, someone has to define what *great* means, and that
process is not always fair or effective.

Gordon Korman, a children's author who consistently produces books with
high boy appeal, is fond of asking audiences to consider how many books there
are on the Newbery Medal list with an extremely slim plot element—namely,

the death of a beloved dog—compared to truly funny books. Korman based an entire book on this concept, *No More Dead Dogs* (Hyperion, 2000). Most of us could recognize many of the books considered to be among the best books for kids with this incredibly thin plot element. Consider *Sounder,* by William H. Armstrong, which won the Newbery Medal in 1970. *Old Yeller,* by Fred Gipson won a Newbery Honor in 1957. *Where the Red Fern Grows,* by Wilson Rawls, should count twice since two dogs meet their mortal end in that book. More recently Sherman Alexie's *The Absolutely True Diary of a Part-Time Indian* won a National Book Award in 2008, and *The Higher Power of Lucky,* by Susan Patron, featuring a doggy death in the opening pages, won the Newbery Medal in 2007.

There wasn't a single Newbery Medal winner that most people would classify as humor until 2012, when Jack Gantos's *Dead End in Norvelt* won. There aren't any sports books. The last nonfiction title to win was *Lincoln: A Photobiography* by Russell Freedman in 1988. Before that, you would have to go back to *Daniel Boone* by James Daugherty, which won in 1940. Of the forty-four books to win Newbery Medals or Newbery Honor Awards from 2003 to 2012, only four were nonfiction, and none won the medal itself.

The first book of gothic horror to win a Newbery was *The Graveyard Book* by Neil Gaiman, in 2009, but there have been two books of poetry that won in the past twenty years, three books on death, two about runaways, two about orphans, and three about depressions (that is, the economic kind; depression of the psychological kind seems almost universal).

James Howe sums up this idea in his satire for children, *Screaming Mummies of the Pharaoh's Tomb II* (Atheneum Books for Young Readers, 2003). Two of his characters, both happening to be dogs, are collaborating on a book, but they can't agree on what kind of book to write. Delilah, the female dog, tries to explain to Howie, the male dog, what would give the book the best chance to win a Newbony Award: "Books that are sad and take place a long time ago. It also helps if the characters are poor and somebody dies, or if the main character, usually a child and preferably an orphan, goes on a long journey. Alone. Oh, and it should be a book girls will like."[37]

> As a person, like many of you, who enjoys reading nearly everything, it's easy to pathologize boys who have reading preferences so different than mine.
>
> —Sandra Lingo, school librarian, in *Library Media Connection*[38]

Whenever we push boys to read "good" books, "real" books, or "the best" books, we have to remember that someone chose that book, and that someone usually wasn't a 10-year-old boy. The Newbery Medal, and so many awards like it, are seldom given to books of the type that appeal to large numbers of boys. Why? Are fiction writers just better than nonfiction writers, since they win most awards for the best in children's literature? Or is there a bias at work?

The real danger is that boys see the types of books that win awards, that make it into school curriculums or onto summer reading lists, and when they don't see anything that appeals to them, they believe they must be bad readers. Boys' reading has value because boys find value in it. As a parent, you may be the only adult in your son's reading life that will honor that.

> I think the key with most young boys is to get to know them personally and find books that fit them. Then, make sure you keep on a theme while branching out their genres so they don't get stuck in the whole "the only book I've ever liked was . . ." mentality.
>
> —Katherine Landau Wright, teacher

To those who worry that boys' reading is too narrow, too restricted by gender stereotypes, researcher William Brozo argues, "Concern for listless and struggling male readers must take precedence for teacher and parents alike."[39] And here is the good news: a survey of successful teen boy readers showed their reading choices match the types that I have described and that poorer readers preferred, with the exception of magazines and humor.[40] Those exceptions may prove the rule. The two types of boys' literature that the successful readers didn't choose are the ones most associated with stress. The poorer readers need their magazines and funny books for reassurance. Reading boys' literature can lead to good boy readers.

The point is not that boys should be allowed to read anything no matter how worthless it is, just so long as they are reading. If that is what you believe, you will almost certainly transmit that attitude in some way to the boys you are trying to help, further convincing them that they are bad readers. They are not. The point is not that boys read bad books, it is that the books that boys find value in thereby have value. The fact that you or your son's teacher do not see the value doesn't matter; you are not the target audience. You aren't a 12-year-old boy.

Big Question: Should Boys Read Girl Books?

Should you encourage your boy to read stereotypically girl books in order to expand his understanding of gender roles and to avoid sexism? We certainly would like to expose students to many different types of reading. The problem comes in the compulsion. If we are encouraging kids to read diversely, then we should be less didactic, or at least allow some choice as to which diverse reading they would like to attempt. If the goal is to improve reading itself, then reading broadly really doesn't matter. William Brozo, an expert in the field of curriculum reading, suggests that teachers would do well to help struggling students identify with texts that are already familiar to them.[41] It only makes sense. Boys already gravitate toward texts that have some meaning for them.

Researcher Sean Cavazos-Kottke points out, "A consistent theme in the literature on reading instruction for the gifted and talented is the importance of personal interest as a significant attitude towards reading . . . Most scholarship on building reading programs for the gifted recommends that gifted readers be given some freedom . . . by self-selecting personally interesting materials."[42] He then suggests that if this is good for the gifted, it should be offered to all.

Choice is the goal, so you really shouldn't be dictating what your son reads anyway. When faced with the "I don't want to read anything" situation, at the library or the bookstore, the best approach is to create a pile of different books that your son can choose from. There is nothing wrong with putting some prototypically girl books in the pile, so long as you are not giving that specific book to read.

You can also look for those books that truly break the lines between what you would call boy books and girl books. Experts call these *crossover books*, and they are worth their weight in gold. These are books such as the Harry Potter series by J. K. Rowling, *The Giver* by Lois Lowry, and *Maniac Magee* by Jerry Spinelli. These not only add some diversity to the standard fare, but they give boys something to read in common with others, which we will look at in the next chapter.

NOTES

1. Kathy Sanford, Heather Blair, and Raymond Chodzinski, "A Conversation about Boys and Literacy," *Teaching and Learning*, Spring 2007, 5.

2. Teri S. Lesesne, *Naked Reading: Uncovering What Tweens Need to Become Lifelong Readers* (Stenhouse, 2006), 26.

3. Donald D. Pottorff, Deborah Phelps-Zientarski, and Michelle E. Skovera, "Gender Perceptions of Elementary and Middle School Students about Literacy at Home and School," *Journal of Research and Development in Education*, Summer 1996, 203.

4. Jon Fine, "Where the Boys Aren't," *Businessweek*, November 7, 2005, 24.

5. Patrick Jones and Dawn Cartwright Fiorelli, "Overcoming the Obstacle Course: Teenage Boys and Reading," *Teacher Librarian*, February 2003, 9.

6. Christina Hoff Sommers, *The War against Boys* (Simon and Schuster, 2000), 164.

7. Jones and Fiorelli, "Overcoming the Obstacle Course," 9.

8. Catherine Sheldrick Ross, Lynne (E. F.) McKechnie, and Paulette M. Rothbauer, *Reading Matters: What the Research Reveals about Reading, Libraries, and Community* (Libraries Unlimited, 2006), 19.

9. Michael O. Tunnell and James S. Jacobs, "Series Fiction and Young Readers," *Booklist*, September 15, 2005, 64.

10. Jonathan Gottschall, *The Storytelling Animal: How Stories Make Us Human* (Houghton Mifflin, 2012), 53–54.

11. Ross, McKechnie, and Rothbauer, *Reading Matters*, 200–201.

12. Gottschall, *The Storytelling Animal*, 53–54.

13. Alison M. G. Follos, *Reviving Reading: School Library Programming, Author Visits and Books That Rock!* (Libraries Unlimited, 2006), 10.

14. Judith A. Morley and Sandra E. Russell, "Making Literature Meaningful: A Classroom/Library Partnership," in *Battling Dragons: Issues and Controversy in Children's Literature* (Heinemann, 1995), 260.

15. Donna Lester Taylor, "'Not Just Boring Stories': Reconsidering the Gender Gap for Boys," *Journal of Adolescent and Adult Literacy*, December 2004/January 2005, 294.

16. Karen Dillon, "No Girls Allowed: Men Bond over Books," *Roanoke Times*, August 3, 2007, C1.

17. Roy Doiron, "Boy Books, Girl Books," *Teacher Librarian*, February 2003, 14.

18. Jeffrey D. Wilhelm and Michael Smith, "Asking the Right Questions: Literate Lives of Boys," *Reading Teacher*, May 2005, 788.

19. Michael Gurian and Patricia Henley, with Terry Trueman, *Boys and Girls Learn Differently! A Guide for Teachers and Parents* (Jossey-Bass, 2001), 49.

20. Gottschall, *The Storytelling Animal*, 66.

21. Greg Toppo, "Funny, but Boys Do Read," *USA Today*, July 6, 2005, Life, 8D.

22. Wilhelm and Smith, "Asking the Right Questions," 788.

23. Robert Fulghum, *It Was on Fire When I Lay Down on It* (Villard, 1989), 217.

24. Taylor, "'Not Just Boring Stories,'" 293.

25. Wilhelm and Smith, "Asking the Right Questions," 788.

26. Sean Cavazos-Kottke, "Five Readers Browsing: The Reading Interests of Talented Middle School Boys," *Gifted Child Quarterly*, Spring 2006, 144.

27. Gurian and Henley, *Boys and Girls Learn Differently*, 49.

28. Anita Gandolfo, *Faith and Fiction: Christian Literature in America Today* (Praeger, 2007), 2–8.

29. Melanie C. Duncan, "A Born-Again Genre," *Library Journal*, February 15, 2012, 27.

30. Gandolfo, *Faith and Fiction*, 113.

31. Duncan, "A Born-Again Genre," 26.

32. Gandolfo, *Faith and Fiction*, 90.

33. Jana Riess, "Christian YA Fiction Still Finding Its Footing," *Publishers Weekly*, August 15, 2011, 31.

34. Gandolfo, *Faith and Fiction*, 101.

35. B. Pirie, *Teenage Boys and High School English* (Heinemann, 2002), 82.

36. Joanne Ujiie and Stephen Krashen, "Are Prize-Winning Books Popular among Children? An Analysis of Public Library Circulation," *Knowledge Quest*, January/February 2006, 35.

37. James Howe, *Screaming Mummies of the Pharaoh's Tomb II* (Atheneum Books for Young Readers, 2003), 6.

38. Sandra Lingo, "The All Guys Book Club: Where Boys Take the Risk to Read," *Library Media Connection*, April/May 2007, 25.

39. William G. Brozo, *To Be a Boy, To Be a Reader* (International Reading Association, 2002), 19.

40. Cavazos-Kottke, "Five Readers Browsing," 144.

41. William G. Brozo, "Bridges to Literacy for Boys," *Educational Leadership*, September 2006, 71–72.

42. Cavazos-Kottke, "Five Readers Browsing," 133.

With Whom Boys Read

Big Question: Single-Gender Education?

A 2005 Kaiser Family Foundation survey found that the average American child spent six and a half hours per day watching television, using computers, or engaged in other electronic activities.[1] Douglas A. Gentile, an Iowa State University psychologist, reports that among third- to fifth-grade rural and suburban kids, girls play video games six hours per week, and boys play thirteen hours per week.[2] These are numbers that make most parents, teachers, and others concerned with the welfare of children shake with fear.

But why are we concerned about screen time? One common answer is isolation: children—and boys so much more than girls—spend too much time in a dark basement all by themselves engaged in electronic entertainment. But is that really the problem?

Video games today are largely interactive. Boys will often argue, with some justification, that they make more friends online in multiplayer games than they would ever make in the so-called real world. Thanks to social networking sites, their virtual communities are vastly larger than their face-to-face communities.

Do you know what boys really find isolating? Reading. And that is the real problem. Boys increasingly seem to see reading as solitary, sedentary, and feminized. Can you think of three things less appealing to a 12-year-old boy? When we are concerned about how much time boys spend in front of a screen instead of reading, we should ask why they spend time in front of a screen instead of reading.

Social Networking and Online Reading

There are fifteen novels based on the World of Warcraft online multiplayer game. Do you think very many people who don't play the game are reading them? There are also books within the game that can be read only in the virtual world that explain the history and culture of the online worlds.[3]

Robert D. Putnam's book *Bowling Alone* bemoans the fact that we now do in isolation what we once did together. Are our kids bowling alone at their video game consoles? No, they are gaming together. In 2011 there were twelve million players on World of Warcraft, more than the population of Nicaragua and Norway combined.[4]

Am I going to argue that screen time is just as good as reading time for our boys? Of course not. But I think we need to look at the on screen reading our boys do a bit differently if we want boys to see reading differently. Texts, web pages, video game instructions, online chat, instant messages—they all add up to reading. If boys are spending that much time online, then reading is happening, and that reading is not happening alone. All this communication involves other people; are you one of them?

I am about to argue that we adults need to be a part of boys' reading, that it is something we should share. That means, first and foremost, honoring the reading that boys do. That won't always be easy, and boys will want to engage in this type of reading mostly with their peers. That doesn't mean you can't do it too.

I personally love the game of chess and teach it to hundreds of people every year. I love the social aspects of the game, the face-to-face time with other people. Consequently, I hate to play on a computer, even if the computer is just a communication tool and the opponent I am playing is a real person. But I teach kids, mostly boys, and they tend to love the computer. So I have learned of late to play some of them online on a site called Chess.com, complete with a chat function that we can use to type in comments, questions, and yes, trash talk.

How do you connect with boys and reading online? One way to start is by joining together a social network site designed for readers, such as Goodreads .com. It is an interactive book journal where users can keep track of the books they are reading, want to read, and have read. They can rate books and review them, and all this is shared with "friends" like any other social networking site.

They can add friends, see what they are reading, and let the computer give them a score on how well their friends' reading tastes match up with their own. Best of all, with a click of a button they can connect with many of the authors of the books they rate.

It isn't a live action shooting game, but it is online, connected to reading, and something you can share with a boy. It engages you with his reading life. Boys need that, because when it comes to reading, too many of our boys are bowling alone.

Role Modeling

Three out of every four teachers in American schools are female.[5] That is bad for role modeling, but not devastating. What really hurts is that 91 percent of elementary school teachers are female. And don't shrug and say that is how it has always been. In 1981, 18 percent of elementary teachers were male.[6] We have cut the number of male elementary teachers in half in thirty years. Similar situations exist in preschools, daycare centers, and story hour at the local public library. For most boys, everyone who teaches him to read is female.

Professor Thomas Dee of Swarthmore College looked at the success of twenty-five thousand students in science, social studies, and English based on the gender of their teachers. Boys did indeed fare better with male teachers and girls with female teachers. Dee believes at least some of that discrepancy comes from the fact that boys' behavior is seen as a bigger problem by female teachers, and 83 percent of the English teachers in his survey were female.[7]

> I am delighted that my children like to read, especially because it is not a big pastime for my husband. He is a little baffled sometimes at the way the rest of us will get absorbed in our books.
> —Tara Tuller Dadd, mother

It gets worse. Most boys don't see men read. That doesn't mean men don't read, just that most men tend to read in isolation. Whenever I speak on the topic, I ask audiences to shout out the answer to a simple question: Where is the proper place for men to read? I am never disappointed. The audience always shouts back, "The bathroom." A stereotype, yes, but the joke is so universal that it must contain a kernel of truth. After all, I get the same answer in the North, South, and Midwest, and on the West Coast. I asked the question in Korea and was greeted with laughter. Too many men read in isolation, where boys can't see them.

Women don't read in isolation; they read in book groups. A study of 350 book groups in the United Kingdom found that more than two thirds were all female, about a quarter were mixed, and only 4 percent were all male.[8] Why? Look at how we do book clubs. Usually, everybody reads the same book. It is usually fiction, and we sit around and talk about the characters. Sound like anything most men would be interested in? If Dad wouldn't be caught dead at a meeting of an Oprah Book Club, why do we think Junior would be any happier? Sadly, this isn't just how we run book groups; this is how almost every English class in America approaches books.

I am a book club junkie, but at every book group I have ever attended, someone has commented on me being male. Why? Because I am always the only one. We need to convince men to read in public, because boys are growing up with the impression that men do not read at all. At best they are learning to read in isolation as well, and anything we do in concert with others we will do better than if we do it alone. After all, that is why we have study buddies, diet buddies, and exercise buddies.

Book Clubs for Boys

Book groups often appeal more to girls than boys, but that is usually because they are held at school or in the library, they look a lot like classroom discussions in English class, and of course, the boys are usually grossly outnumbered by girls. One way to build camaraderie among boys as readers is to have a book club that really honors the way boys read. Yes, you can host a book club with your son and a few of his friends, and maybe include parents. Dads especially might find this a great activity. The real trick is to make your book club look as different as possible from the book groups that boys are used to seeing.

Holding a book club in your home, or rotating through the homes of the boys involved, is a good enough idea, but stretch a little. How about holding it in a coffee shop or ice cream parlor? You have immediately made the club a bit more exciting and less like a Cub Scout den meeting. Better yet, move the discussion to interesting places that have some connection to the book. I owe that idea to the Children's Literature Council of Southern California. They move their entire conference to sites that connect with whatever the year's theme is. When they invited me to speak on boys and reading, they held the conference at the Petersen Auto Museum. If talking about boys and reading a floor above the original Batmobile was unbelievably cool, imagine how engaged boys would be there after reading Gary Paulsen's *The Car* (Houghton Mifflin, 1994).

Last night I had my first "all new" boys book group! No more sitting in chairs in a circle to talk about the characters and how that makes them feel! I had already picked a book that they had been reading; Lunch Lady and the League of Librarians . . . I tried to come up with a hands-on activity. I am guessing you know the Lunch Lady series but in it, the Lunch Lady and Betty use kitchen items as gadgets to fight off and capture the evil villains. So I brought in items from my home and piled them on the floor and told the boys to take some items and come up with their own gadgets and if they wanted to, add some story ideas, they could to. They spent about 20 minutes drawing and writing their items and of course playing with the items. Then we sat on the floor and talked about them. It was interesting that the last boy to talk made all his as defensive weapons/items. The other boys were all out to get the bad guy.

But here is the good stuff; One of the parents that attended was a guy! One boy had come early to check out other similar books because he liked the comic book style so much (and his mom, who is a friend of mine, said he is a reluctant reader). The other Lunch Lady books that I brought to book group all went home with the boys. They all participated and had original ideas. As they were leaving I overheard one boy tell his mom that he had fun!
—Jennifer Whitehead, children's librarian

Wherever you hold the book club, avoid setting up chairs around a table or in a circle. Girls tend to speak face-to-face; boys often speak best shoulder-to-shoulder. Speaking face-to-face has an aura of intimacy. Speaking shoulder-to-shoulder implies shared activity, even if you are doing nothing. Do not put kids facing each other and expect boys to open up. You may not want to sit them down at all. This works well if the book club meets at sites connected with the book: sports events, museums, police stations, anywhere. Often when attempting to do a boy-focused book discussion, we discuss the book and then do some engaging activity. By then you have already lost. Do the activity, and let the discussion arise by itself.

The books chosen will affect boys' response to a book group. Many boys respond well to fantasy, humor, action-adventure, and especially nonfiction, seldom included in English class discussions and school or library book groups. An all-men's reading club in Roanoke, Virginia, discovered that half the books they chose were nonfiction, and the club was long-standing and very successful.[9] If adult men read that way, you can be pretty sure boys will enjoy the same approach.

These types of reading—what I described in chapter 4, "What Boys Read"—are a generalization. To best match the needs of the members, allow them to choose. Rotate the job of nominating books among the members and have them vote on which book they will read. Such choice is important; it selects books that actually interest the readers and assures them they have control of their reading. And they do not all have to read the same book. That is a belief we have adopted from classroom discussions, and it has no place in a club devoted to fun reading. Once or twice a year at least, have everyone read a book of his choice and present it to the group. This can inspire extra reading in all the members and become a way of choosing books for the coming sessions.

Finally, distance a book group from classroom discussions. They are not a way of assessing kids' reading. Fight the urge to needle them with questions to make sure they really read the book. They are there talking about the book—that is enough. In fact, you don't have to talk about the book itself at all; just reinforce the plot through fun and engaging activities. Here is an example of a nondiscussion book meeting. It's called the "Loser Olympics."

Start with the book *Loser* by Jerry Spinelli (HarperTrophy, 2003). *Loser* is about Donald Zinkoff, a boy who is, without a doubt, a loser. This is no Disney-type ugly duckling story where the character thinks he is a loser but we find out in the end there is a hero within. Donald really is a loser. He wears a four-foot-tall giraffe hat to kindergarten. His handwriting is so bad it is unreadable. He idolizes his dad and wants to be a mailman just like him. He cannot play any sport to save his life, despite his unquenchable excitement to try. His teacher, in an attempt at inclusion, makes Donald the anchor leg of the relay race at field day. Donald is handed a huge lead, runs with arms and legs flailing, and goes nowhere. Everyone passes him and Donald's class comes in last. Donald Zinkoff is a loser.

A standard book discussion would probably start with the question "Is Donald Zinkoff a loser?" The answer from just about any boy would be, "Oh, totally. Can we have cookies now?"

Host the Loser Olympics instead, a series of events based on the book. Gather large boots from the community: work boots, waders, galoshes, whatever will fit over a kid's shoes. Make each participant pull a pair of boots over his shoes and make them run a course around the room. Make sure there are at least a few sharp curves. The kids will run flailing like Donald Zinkoff, with similar results.

Duct tape oven mitts over the kids' hands and have them throw footballs to one another in pairs, starting inches apart. They can hand the football to each other from there. Some will still drop the ball, and those teams are out. Then have each child step back and toss the ball. Keep having them step back until only one team is left that has not fumbled themselves out of the competition.

Have a writing contest using everybody's weak hand; watch out for lefties who try to cheat. Print a quotation and give it to the first player on each team to copy. They then give the paper to the next team member, who must copy it again, and so on through the whole team. The team whose final product is closest to the original wins.

There are no limits to the number of events you can host in a Loser Olympics. Pick any scene from the book and use your imagination. The key is how involved each member of the group is, and how many colorful ribbons you can give out for prizes.

Another great approach to a boys' book club is to make it experiment-based. There are plenty of books out there full of fun experiments. Reading these together and voting on the experiment to do helps build the social side of reading, and it honors the active, inquisitive nature of boys.

> ## Experiment and Activity Books for Boys' Book Clubs
>
> Cindy Blobaum. *Awesome Snake Science! 40 Activities for Learning about Snakes.* Chicago Review Press, 2012.
>
> Ken Denmead. *The Geek Dad Book for Aspiring Mad Scientists: The Coolest Experiments and Projects for Science Fairs and Family Fun.* Gotham, 2011.
>
> William Gurstelle. *Backyard Ballistics.* Expanded edition. Chicago Review Press, 2012.
>
> Theresa Luu and Mirela Marku. *Mother and Son Kitchen Book Club: Stories and Recipes for Hungry Minds.* Mother and Sons, 2012.
>
> Dave Reay. *Your Planet Needs You! A Kid's Guide to Going Green.* Macmillan, 2009.

You have to look at books in ways that speak to boys. Allow for a certain amount of physicality in connection with reading, connect boys' reading with the things that interest them, and lead boys to books by modeling a love for reading.

Big Question: Single-Gender Education?

Parents often ask me if they should think about putting their sons into all-boy classrooms or schools. The subject of male-only schools and classrooms often draws passionate opposition, but we should remember that in the 1990s, schools often instituted all-female math and science classes to overcome the math and science gap. It made sense. Girls fell behind in these areas not because of any lack of innate ability, but because the way these classes were taught did not speak to many girls. Single-gender classes allowed teachers to teach in a way that did speak to girls. This same approach may be applied to boys and reading.

Of course there is a long history of private and parochial schools that are entirely single gender. These schools may be the best environment for some boys, and they are voluntary, so few object to their existence. Then there is public education. Many contend that separate is inherently unequal and oppose any separation of boys and girls. But then there are the long-term, obvious problems so many boys have with reading. There need to be new approaches and at least options. Clearly, large numbers of boys fail to become readers the way we do things now, so boys and their parents should be able to choose options that may produce better results.

In the case of public schools, we are usually looking at individual classes for boys, not entire schools. Twin Ridge Elementary School in Mount Airy, Maryland, had voluntary males-only reading classes for fourth and fifth graders in 2005.[10] Thornton Academy, a privately run school that operates as a public school for three towns in Maine, introduced an all-boys freshman English class to address struggling readers in 2007–2008. Lyseth Elementary School in Portland, Maine, segregated two of its fourth-grade classes by gender for some subjects. Dorchester, Massachusetts; New Haven, Connecticut; and Hartford, Connecticut all have had single-gender public school classes.[11] The Walter C. Cunningham School for Excellence in Waterloo, Iowa, had three single-gender classrooms in 2006, an all-boys second grade and one third grade for each gender. There were 211 single gender classrooms in 2006.[12] There were eleven public schools in six states entirely single-gender in 2004, and 366 public schools across the country offered some form of single-sex instruction in 2008.[13]

There is some evidence that these classrooms do a good job of addressing boys' reading problems. Woodward Elementary School in DeLand, Florida, found that 37 percent of their boys in coed classes passed the state writing test, but 86 percent of those in all-boy classes passed.[14] Such classrooms give an opportunity for a very different learning experience for boys. At the Cunningham School for Excellence, a grade school in Waterloo, Iowa, for grades pre-K through 5, students in all-boy classes "are not required to sit still and be quiet. They are welcome to stand or sit or curl up under their desks, or jump up and down if they like." Their teacher reported that the boys were not only succeeding, they were thriving.[15] Similar all-boy classes with almost unrecognizable classroom structures were reported at the Hardey Prep, a parochial elementary school in Chicago, and public schools in Foley, Alabama, and Seattle, Washington.[16] Phi Beta Kappa has given at least tentative approval, saying that single-gender classrooms might particularly benefit minority and low-income students, and that such classes at the high school level may reduce the dropout rate.[17]

It is worth noting that simply segregating boys is unlikely to produce much in the way of results. In Canada, "boys-only programs struggled and were terminated because the schools had not thought through why they had put them together in the first place . . . They simply put a class full of junior high boys together, picked a few boy books, and did little else differently." Boys-only classes were seen only as balancing the girls-only math and science classes that had existed for years.[18] The goal must be to use the single-gender atmosphere to teach reading in ways that speak to boys and to feature reading that will appeal to them. It would be an equally big mistake to simply recreate a remedial class as a single-gender class. The expectation must be that all-boy classes will produce better results. Jeff Ferguson, who taught the all-boy class at the Cunningham School in Iowa, is uncompromising with his simple goal: college for every one of his boys.[19] That is the approach to take.

You clearly don't want to force boys into single-gender classes. But if the option exists, it is worth considering. Ask yourself, and your son and the teachers involved, if there is a difference in how the classes are taught, or if they are just separating boys and girls to avoid distractions. Then ask if the particular classroom approach might help your son's particular reading issues. One size cannot fit all when it comes to education. That is clear from the results we see now with boys and reading. Some boys will benefit from an all-boy reading class, and some won't. The more options that exist for boys, the more chance there is that any given boy will find an atmosphere that fits his needs. Whatever the decision, the boy himself should have a large say.

NOTES

1. Marilyn Elias, "Electronic World Swallows Up Kids' Time, Study Finds," *USA Today*, March 10, 2005, A1.

2. Peg Tyre, *The Trouble with Boys: A Surprising Report Card on Our Sons, Their Problems at School, and What Parents and Educators Must Do* (Crown Publishers, 2008), 189.

3. Jonathan Gottschall, *The Storytelling Animal: How Stories Make Us Human* (Houghton Mifflin, 2012), 193.

4. Ibid.

5. William G. Brozo, "Gender and Reading Literacy," *Reading Today*, February/March 2005, 18.

6. Tyre, *The Trouble with Boys*, 126.

7. Richard Whitmire, *Why Boys Fail: Saving Our Sons from an Educational System That's Leaving Them Behind* (American Management Association, 2010), 86.

8. Catherine Sheldrick Ross, Lynne (E. F.) McKechnie, and Paulette M. Rothbauer, *Reading Matters: What the Research Reveals about Reading, Libraries, and Community* (Libraries Unlimited, 2006), 227.

9. Karen Dillon, "No Girls Allowed: Men Bond over Books," *Roanoke Times*, August 3, 2007, C1.

10. "School Experiments with Same-Sex Reading Groups," *Curriculum Review*, April 2005, 8.

11. "Educators Keep an Eye on Boys-Only Experiment at Thornton Academy," *Associated Press*, February 10, 2008.

12. Mary Ellen Flannery, "No Girls Allowed," *NEA Today*, April 2006, www.nea.org/home/12376.htm.

13. Liz Austin, "More U.S. Schools Segregating Sexes," *Associated Press*, August 24, 2004; "Educators Keep an Eye on Boys-Only Experiment," *Associated Press*.

14. Flannery, "No Girls Allowed."

15. Leonard Sax, "The Boy Problem," *School Library Journal*, September 2007, 41.

16. Ibid.

17. Flannery, "No Girls Allowed."

18. Kathy Sanford, Heather Blair, and Raymond Chodzinski, "A Conversation about Boys and Literacy," *Teaching and Learning*, Spring 2007, 11.

19. Flannery, "No Girls Allowed."

In Closing

Although the current results suggest that [kindergarten] teachers should be aware of male deficits in early reading skill development, they also suggest that these differences are small, temporary, and surmountable.
—Jaime L. Below et al., in *School Psychology Review*[1]

Do we need to always worry about boys and reading? Only while boys' reading lags so far behind girls' reading. Donalyn Miller, in *The Book Whisperer*, gives virtually no mention of gender. Stephen Krashen doesn't mention boys, girls, or gender in his foundational work *The Power of Reading*. These two books that underpin the idea of free, independent reading give the promise that this approach could obliterate the boys' reading problem once and for all.

Traditional language arts instruction . . . is merely a test, a test that privileged children, who grow up with books, pass and that less fortunate children fail . . . and like victims of child abuse, they blame themselves.
—Stephen Krashen, *The Power of Reading*[2]

Sadly, free and independent reading is not happening in most schools, and hence the depressing statistics peppering this book. Parents need to create this world for their sons if they want boys to become successful readers. But it is more important to make your son a lifelong reader. Passing standardized reading tests tells you little to nothing about what kind of reader your son is. Grades in English and other subjects say more, but shouldn't be your first concern.

> Literacy is not something that is acquired once and for all in school and then, like an inoculation, lasts a lifetime. Practice is continually required.
> —Catherine Ross, Lynne McKechnie, and
> Paulette Rothbauer, *Reading Matters*[3]

Boys who read just to get through school and get the grades they need to pass have managed to master content. Great. Unfortunately, schools can teach only so much content, and the content that your son needs will change year after year. What you need to do to really prepare a boy for the world he will face is to make reading a habit he will practice, willingly, for the rest of his life. Experts warn us that children growing up today will not hold one job or even one career for life, but will likely move through a number of careers. What they need to learn now is how to learn later, and that means becoming a reader.

> My older son credits his love of recreational reading to the fact that his dad and I were both readers. When he was in college, he was the only one of his friends who read for pleasure.
> —Ellen Burnham Knowlton, public librarian

And what makes boys readers? Never discount the importance of one or two people in their lives. I love to remind teachers and librarians that this is the most important—and most rewarding—part of their job: to influence one child at a time in a habit that will enrich and engage them for the rest of their lives. Schools do not create readers. Libraries don't create readers. These are systems designed to serve a role, not change lives. They give certain people a chance to make a difference, but it is the people themselves who make the difference. No teacher or librarian has the opportunity to affect a boy the way a parent or close friend can.

It is a matter of hours, pure and simple. You spend more time with the boys in your life than any one teacher can. Support boys and their reading. Encourage them and give them the freedom and the tools to drive their own reading. But more than anything, be a role model. If you spend more time engaged in determining what he should read than you yourself spend reading, then he is going to see this as hypocrisy, and you have lost him. Show him that you control your own reading and that it is an important part of your life, and he will do likewise.

As you can see, the answers to boys' reading problems aren't brain science, though there is brain science behind them. Boys are individuals; but just as there are reading problems common to huge numbers of boys, there are strategies for addressing those problems that can help large numbers of boys as well.

Recognize the differences common between boys and girls.

Honor the lag in brain development that often puts boys at odds with expectations that have nothing to do with their future as readers.

Know why boys read, and what the psychological payoff is for your boy; you are more likely to encourage him that way.

Be accepting of how boys read.

Don't judge boys' reading; try to understand it so you can be a supportive guide to reading.

Be with boys when they read, and make sure they see people reading, not just hear about it endlessly.

And always remember the two key factors: lower the stress on boys when it comes to reading, and put the power to choose their reading in their hands. These things will make reading a lifelong habit. You aren't teaching boys to read; you are making them readers. Do that, and they can make themselves anything they want to be.

NOTES

1. Jamie Below et al., "Gender Differences in Early Literacy: Analysis of Kindergarten through Fifth-Grade Dynamic Indicators of Basic Early Literacy Skills Probes," *School Psychology Review*, 2010, 254.

2. Stephen D. Krashen, *The Power of Reading: Insights from the Research*, 2nd ed. (Libraries Unlimited, 2004), 38.

3. Catherine Sheldrick Ross, Lynne (E. F.) McKechnie, and Paulette M. Rothbauer, *Reading Matters: What the Research Reveals about Reading, Libraries, and Communities* (Libraries Unlimited, 2006), 4.

Annotated Booklists

Some Recent Books to Catch Boy Readers

These titles were published since 2009 or are recent series that were still being published after 2009. Boys are often very sensitive to the age of their books. It is a confidence issue; they have been handed so many older books that are severely dated.

The lists are broken down by elementary, middle school, and high school for convenience's sake, but do not take these divisions too seriously. Boys will read well above and below what is expected of their age, and it is more important to get something in their hands that appeals to them than to match up reading levels.

This section contains annotated lists of fiction and nonfiction; for elementary, middle school, and high school boys; arranged by title. The following section contains lists of titles from these master lists, including some by genre and some by subject. Many of these lists include both fiction and nonfiction. Remember that boys often read nonfiction the way that we expect kids to read fiction. So books listed under "Military" can be true histories as well as historical fiction.

Of course, not all books fall neatly into one list or another. The lines between fantasy, gothic, and science fiction are especially blurred these days. And is a funny book about robots considered humor or science fiction? Any kind of book can be done in comics form, so where do you put a comic strip history of the United States? The answer, of course, is in both places. Don't worry too much about any pigeonholing; these lists are meant to be a starting point. Many boys are loyal readers of a genre ("I only read funny books" or "I only read fantasy"), but many will welcome genre-bending works, sometimes called *mash-ups*, that leave them within a comfortable genre but still offer something new and different.

Elementary Nonfiction

Afraid of the Water (series)
Bearport, 2010.

1. *Blue-Ringed Octopus: Small but Deadly.* By Natalie Lunis.
2. *Box Jellyfish: Killer Tentacles.* By Natalie Lunis.
3. *Moray Eel: Dangerous Teeth.* By Meish Goldish.
4. *Portuguese Man-of-War: Floating Misery.* By Natalie Lunis.
5. *Shark: The Shredder.* By Meish Goldish.
6. *Stonefish: Needles of Pain.* By Meish Goldish.

ANIMALS; HI/LO; SCIENCE Snakes . . . snakes underwater . . . huge snakes underwater, with big teeth that curve in so no prey can escape. They blend into their surroundings so you don't know they are there, until it's too late! Moray eels are just one of the nightmare creatures lurking in the deep in the series Afraid of the Water!

Baby Mammoth Mummy: Frozen in Time!
A Prehistoric Animal's Journey into the 21st Century
By Christopher Sloan with Bernard Buigues. Photographs by Francis Latreille. National Geographic, 2011.

ANIMALS; SCIENCE Look inside a real mammoth with space-age technology. Gaze across the ancient mammoth steppes. Starting from the discovery of a perfectly preserved baby woolly mammoth and working backward to the last ice age, National Geographic does what it does best: opens new worlds with amazing visuals.

Barnum's Bones: How Barnum Brown Discovered the Most Famous Dinosaur in the World

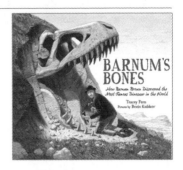

By Tracy Fern. Illustrated by Boris Kulikov. Farrar, Straus and Giroux, 2012.

ANIMALS; BIOGRAPHY, AUTOBIOGRAPHY, AND MEMOIR; SCIENCE What boy doesn't love learning about dinosaurs? Today that means reading books about them, but Barnum Brown lived when the books were still being written. If he wanted to learn about a new dinosaur, he had to go dig it out of the ground. And that's what he did, all over the world, until he found the king of all dinosaurs.

Big Cats: In Search of Lions, Leopards, Cheetahs, and Tigers

By Steve Bloom. Thames and Hudson, 2012.

ANIMALS; SCIENCE The pictures in this book on the world's great cats are just stunning. There are words, too, with facts about the animals, but the pictures . . . Oh, and there is much to inspire young photographers, but still, the pictures . . . wow.

Biggest, Baddest Book of Beasts

By Anders Hanson and Elissa Mann. ABDO, 2013.

ANIMALS; SCIENCE Big, fast, fanged, venomous, and armed. Right up close. Come face to face with nothing but the beastliest of the beasts.

The Boston Tea Party

By Russell Freedman. Illustrated by Peter Malone. Holiday House, 2012.

HISTORY Can you start a war without soldiers or firing a shot, but with humor, costumes, and what was basically a big party instead? America did it; find out how.

Brothers at Bat: The True Story of an Amazing All-Brother Baseball Team

By Audrey Vernick. Illustrated by Steven Salerno. Clarion, 2012.

BIOGRAPHY, AUTOBIOGRAPHY, AND MEMOIR; SPORTS Acerra playing first, Acerra at second, Acerra at third, and your shortstop is Acerra. Playing outfield, from left to right, is Acerra, Acerra, and Acerra. Acerra is on the mound, and Acerra behind the plate. That's your starting lineup. Stay tuned for the batting order . . . Yeah, that's what you get with a team made up entirely of brothers. That, and a place in the Baseball Hall of Fame.

The Case of the Vanishing Golden Frogs: A Scientific Mystery

By Sandra Markle. Millbrook Press, 2012.

ACTION, ADVENTURE, AND MYSTERY; ANIMALS; SCIENCE Tracking killers doesn't just happen on TV shows or police stations. Scientists had to find the culprit who was killing the Panamanian golden frog before the species was wiped out entirely. See how dedicated detectives tracked down the killer in the jungles of Central America. Spoiler alert! The killer is still at large, but he's been identified, and the frogs have been saved from extinction. For the budding scientist who doesn't want to be trapped in a lab.

Disaster Survivors (series)

Bearport, 2010.

1. *Blitzed by a Blizzard!* By Joyce L. Markovics.
2. *Devastated by a Volcano!* By Stephen Person.
3. *Erased by a Tornado!* By Jessica Rudolph.
4. *Hammered by a Heat Wave!* By Laura DeLallo.
5. *Leveled by an Earthquake!* By Adam Reingold.
6. *Mangled by a Hurricane!* By Miriam Aronin.
7. *Slammed by a Tsunami!* By Miriam Aronin.
8. *Struck by Lightning!* By Stephen Person.

ACTION, ADVENTURE, AND MYSTERY; HI/LO In *Struck by Lightning!*, Person manages to give a great deal of very real information without losing the wonder, the awe, the raw power of nature unleashed in bolts of pure energy that can travel more than twenty miles in the blink of an eye. This is the perfect setting for the big five questions: Who does lightning strike? Where? When? How often? And most important, why? It's all here in a slim volume with some spectacular photography and easily accessible text. Give a kid twenty minutes with this book and he will be running to the computer to find more, diving for another book in the series, or looking for a kite and a key. Bearport Publishing is the home of great nonfiction written at an accessible level, and natural sciences are their specialty.

Dogs on Duty:
Soldiers' Best Friends on the Battlefield and Beyond
By Dorothy Hinshaw Patent. Walker, 2012.

ANIMALS; HISTORY; MILITARY When can a dog be a SEAL? When it is a military working dog! Meet these four-legged heroes and see how they are raised and trained, and how they save lives and serve their country.

Fast Rides (series)
By Michael Sandler. Bearport, 2011.

1. *Dynamic Drag Racers*
2. *Electrifying Eco-Race Cars*
3. *Hot Hot Rods*
4. *Jet-Powered Speed*

HI/LO It's where gearheads, speed freaks, tree huggers, and techno-nuts meet to say . . . "Wow!"

For Liberty: The Story of the Boston Massacre; Addressed to the Inhabitants of America
By Timothy Decker. Calkins Creek, 2009.

HISTORY; MILITARY For those elementary and middle school kids who remember their picture book days as the last time they loved reading, here is a powerful take on a grimly fascinating event. This is "small" history—fifteen minutes that changed the world—and the drama is enhanced by stark, black-and-white illustrations that evoke both David Macaulay and the manga form. Perhaps its greatest gift is to individualize the players, making the tragedy all the more human. This is history that comes alive.

Game-Day Youth (series)
By Suzy Beamer Bohnert. B&B Publishing.

1. *Game-Day Youth: Learning Baseball's Lingo.* 2010.
2. *Game-Day Youth: Learning Basketball's Lingo.* 2011.

SPORTS From the "Game-Day Goddess" comes books on the language of sports for the complete novice. What makes them special? They cover not just the official terms but slang as well. Where else are you going to find a definition of a "ticky-tack foul"? A bit simplistic for the sports buff, but for anybody who wants to sit down next to Dad and watch a game, these are the dictionaries for you.

Ghosts:
A Nonfiction Companion to "A Good Night for Ghosts"
By Mary Pope Osborne and Natalie Pope Boyce. Illustrated by Sal Murdocca. Random House, 2009.

GOTHIC HORROR, SUPERNATURAL, AND SUSPENSE Cases of real death in the form of real ghost stories, highly illustrated and quickly told. Great for those kids already addicted to the Magic Tree House series, and a grand introduction for those who aren't.

An Inside Look at the U.S. Navy SEALs
By Joe Funk. Scholastic, 2011.

HISTORY; MILITARY A first look at the men, machines, weapons, vehicles, and missions of the best of the best elite fighting forces in the world, including a look at how they took down Osama bin Laden.

Just Joking: 300 Hilarious Jokes, Tricky Tongue Twisters, and Ridiculous Riddles
National Geographic, 2012.

Just Joking 2: 300 Hilarious Jokes about Everything, Including Tongue Twisters, Riddles, and More!
National Geographic, 2012.

ANIMALS; HUMOR Jokes, riddles, fun animal facts, and funny pictures of animals telling the jokes—what's not to love?

Leprechauns and Irish Folklore:
A Nonfiction Companion to "Leprechaun in Late Winter"
By Mary Pope Osborne and Natalie Pope Boyce. Illustrated by Sal Murdocca. Random House, 2010.

FANTASY AND MAGICAL REALISM Who needs a story written about some of the best stories ever? Why not just enjoy Irish folklore? Revel in the playful— and sometimes not so playful—deeds of the wee folk, whether meeting to dance beneath the stars, tearing apart houses that were built on fairy roads, or spiriting away their little hoards of gold. Learn how to find that gold, how to lift a fairy spell, and what it means when a banshee wails outside your window.

Mysteries of the Komodo Dragon:
The Biggest, Deadliest Lizard Gives Up Its Secrets
By Marty Crump. Boyds Mills Press, 2010.

ANIMALS; SCIENCE A great transitional book for those boys who loved dinosaur and critter picture books and who now read independently. Mature enough to share with an adult as well.

No Easy Way:
The Story of Ted Williams and the Last .400 Season
By Fred Bowen. Illustrated by Charles S. Pyle. Dutton, 2010.

BIOGRAPHY, AUTOBIOGRAPHY, AND MEMOIR; SPORTS Ted Williams's amazing season has never been matched, but what makes the story special is the character he displayed laying out the whole season when there was nothing left to win, and risking falling below the magic .400 mark. The drama of the final day, the final at bats, makes this a gripping story by a master sports writer. The picture book format makes it accessible for independent readers and for parents to read to their younger sons.

Saving the Baghdad Zoo: A True Story of Hope and Heroes
By Kelly Milner Halls and William Sumner. Greenwillow, 2010.

ANIMALS; MILITARY War destroys lives, and not just human lives. A handful of brave people, led by an American army officer, took on the challenge of saving the animals in zoos all over Baghdad during the Iraq War. With bullets flying around them, they wrangled lions, alligators, and many more animals. Heroes come in some surprising shapes.

Spirit Seeker:
John Coltrane's Musical Journey
By Gary Golio. Paintings by Rudy Gutierrez. Clarion, 2012.

BIOGRAPHY, AUTOBIOGRAPHY, AND MEMOIR John Coltrane was called to heights of faith, raised to mountaintops by music, and driven to depths by loss and addiction. His life swirled like the notes of his saxophone in the chaotic birth of jazz. This book, in a spare forty pages of tight language and lush illustrations, will make you feel the man and his music.

The Work of Heroes: First Responders in Action (series)
Bearport.

1. *Animal Control Officers to the Rescue.* By Meish Goldish. 2013.
2. *Doctors to the Rescue.* By Meish Goldish. 2012.
3. *Firefighters to the Rescue.* By Meish Goldish. 2012.
4. *Paramedics to the Rescue.* By Nancy White. 2012.
5. *Police Officers to the Rescue.* By Nancy White. 2012.
6. *Wildlife Rehabilitators to the Rescue.* By Meish Goldish. 2013.

ACTION, ADVENTURE, AND MYSTERY; BIOGRAPHY, AUTOBIOGRAPHY, AND MEMOIR; HI/LO Real heroes presented as real people. Depicts extraordinary people without sensationalizing them.

X-Moves (series)
By Michael Sandler. Bearport, 2010.

1. *Cool Snowboarders*
2. *Daring BMXers*
3. *Gnarly Skateboarders*
4. *Mighty MotoXers*
5. *Rally Car Dudes*
6. *Super Surfers*

BIOGRAPHY, AUTOBIOGRAPHY, AND MEMOIR; HI/LO; SPORTS For the early gearhead crowd, *Mighty MotoXers* is a quick, highly visual tour of the motocross world. The stop-action photos of every step of a trick are particularly stunning. And that is just the beginning of the daring tricks and amazing photography in this series for the extreme sports fanatic.

Middle School Nonfiction

Adventure Beneath the Sea: Living in an Underwater Science Station
By Kenneth Mallory. Photographs by Brian Skerry. Boyds Mills Press, 2010.

ACTION, ADVENTURE, AND MYSTERY; SCIENCE Dreaming of exploring another world? You don't have to wait until you can fly to Mars; there are unexplored worlds here on Earth. Forget being an astronaut—why not try being an aquanaut?

Albert Einstein and Relativity for Kids: His Life and Ideas with 21 Activities and Thought Experiments

By Jerome Pohlen. Chicago Review Press, 2012.

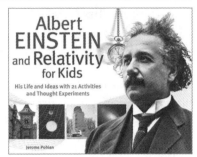

BIOGRAPHY, AUTOBIOGRAPHY, AND MEMOIR; SCIENCE Edwin Hubble, the famous astronomer, was showing a German couple the Mount Wilson Observatory when he told them that this most advanced telescope in the world was used to determine the shape and nature of the universe. The women replied, "Oh, my husband does that on the back of an old envelope." The woman was Elsa Einstein, and her husband was Albert. Albert Einstein was born with a funny-shaped head, out of which would come all the secrets of the universe, the basis of the atomic bomb, a lifelong dedication to passivism, and a brain that would eventually end up in a cookie jar in Kansas. What a ride.

Awesome Snake Science! 40 Activities for Learning about Snakes

By Cindy Blobaum. Chicago Review Press, 2012.

ANIMALS; SCIENCE Here's a book for the real reptile lover, or just the science nut. Written very scientifically but at an accessible level, it honors the serious nature lover. And good news for parents: no real snakes needed!

Blizzard of Glass: The Halifax Explosion of 1917

By Sally M. Walker. Henry Holt, 2011.

HISTORY What is the connection between the city of Halifax in Canada, World War I, and the Christmas tree in Boston, Massachusetts? Two thousand deaths in the largest man-made explosion before the atomic bomb, that's what.

Bomb: The Race to Build—and Steal— the World's Most Dangerous Weapon

By Steve Sheinkin. Roaring Brook, 2012.

HISTORY; MILITARY The atomic bomb would, without doubt, determine the outcome of World War II and shape the world that would follow. America's future depended on building the bomb before the Germans, and keeping the secret away from the Soviets. So the story of the bomb is not just one of scientists unlocking one of nature's greatest secrets, but of daring commando raids and cloak-and-dagger spies that would put James Bond to shame.

Bro-Jitsu: The Martial Art of Sibling Smackdown

By Daniel H. Wilson. Illustrated by Les McClaine. Bloomsbury, 2010.

HUMOR Physical and psychological torture of bratty little brothers and bossy older sisters is part of a grand tradition going back to caveman times. Master the arts of noogies, fake nipples, the hanging spit fake, and the python leg squeeze, then hide this book before your brother finds it and turns this ancient art against you!

Candy Bomber:
The Story of the Berlin Airlift's "Chocolate Pilot"

By Michael O. Tunnell. Charlesbridge, 2010.

BIOGRAPHY, AUTOBIOGRAPHY, AND MEMOIR; HISTORY; MILITARY The U.S. military is, and has long been, about more than winning wars. They also try to win the hearts and minds of peoples they come in contact with around the world, and sometimes we need to be reminded of the best of the U.S. military tradition. The Candy Bomber of the Berlin Airlift is one great example. Also check out *Saving the Baghdad Zoo,* by Kelly Milner Halls and William Sumner.

50 Poisonous Questions: A Book with Bite

By Tanya Lloyd Kyi. Illustrated by Ross Kinnaird. Annick Press, 2011.

ANIMALS; SCIENCE Half this book is about poisons in nature, fangs, warts, and clicking mandibles. Very cool. The other half is about the poisons we humans put into the world and use on one another. Infuriating. All of it is worth the read.

Frederick Douglass for Kids:
His Life and Times with 21 Activities

By Nancy I. Sanders. Chicago Review Press, 2012.

BIOGRAPHY, AUTOBIOGRAPHY, AND MEMOIR; HISTORY "Frederick Douglass was a man of decisions. As a child, he made the decision to learn to read and write because he realized literacy was the path to freedom. When he was a young man, he decided to take freedom into his own hands and escape from slavery. As an abolitionist, he decided to publish his personal story . . . , even though he knew it would endanger his life. And when he had the choice to live in England enjoying peace and equality, he decided to return home . . . and fight for the freedoms of his people." We all need role models to show us the best in people.

Hammerin' Hank Greenberg: Baseball Pioneer
By Shelley Sommer. Calkins Creek, 2011.

BIOGRAPHY, AUTOBIOGRAPHY, AND MEMOIR; SPORTS In the 1930s and 1940s, sports went a long way toward breaking down barriers. We all know about Jackie Robinson, Joe Louis, and Jesse Owens, but few people know the story of Hank Greenberg, the first great Jewish baseball player, who fought through discrimination to win two MVP awards and the respect of a nation for his character, his patriotism, and his home-run swing.

Here There Be Monsters: The Legendary Kraken and the Giant Squid
By H. P. Newquist. Houghton Mifflin, 2010.

ANIMALS; SCIENCE The only thing more exciting than a monster of myth is when the monster turns out to be real. This nonfiction picture book format includes every known picture of the giant and colossal squids, as well as many of the fanciful pictures of the legendary kraken. For everyone who likes real-life adventure stories, as well as those fans of a good creature feature.

HorrorScapes (series)
Bearport, 2011.

1. *Dracula's Dark World.* By Michael Burgan.
2. *Ghostly Alcatraz Island.* By Stephen Person.
3. *Tut's Deadly Tomb.* By Natalie Lunis.
4. *Voodoo in New Orleans.* By Stephen Person.
5. *Witchcraft in Salem.* By Steven L. Stern.

GOTHIC HORROR, SUPERNATURAL, AND SUSPENSE; HI/LO What lurks in the dark places of the world? Ghosts, legends, myths, and things that you wouldn't want to meet under the night sky. Take a tour of the scariest corners of the earth.

How They Croaked: The Awful Ends of the Awfully Famous
By Georgia Bragg. Illustrated by Kevin O'Malley. Walker, 2011.

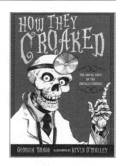

BIOGRAPHY, AUTOBIOGRAPHY, AND MEMOIR; HISTORY The bullet in President Garfield's back missed all vital organs and wouldn't have killed him. The infection from the doctors' prying an eight-inch trench into his back with their fingers trying to find the bullet did him in. Einstein's skull and brain were poached by souvenir hunters before he could be cremated. Napoleon, Caesar, Washington—here are all their bizarre ends.

Invincible Microbe:
Tuberculosis and the Never-Ending Search for a Cure
By Jim Murphy and Alison Blank. Clarion, 2012.

HISTORY; SCIENCE The human race is at war, and has been for thousands of years. More people have died in this war than all the ones ever fought with guns. The enemy? A microbe too small to see. Do you think we won the war against tuberculosis, the greatest of all biological weapons? Think again . . .

Lincoln's Flying Spies:
Thaddeus Lowe and the Civil War Balloon Corps
By Gail Jarrow. Calkins Creek, 2010.

BIOGRAPHY, AUTOBIOGRAPHY, AND MEMOIR; HISTORY; MILITARY How did man first fly? Who made up the first U.S. Air Force? Don't think planes or the Wright brothers, think balloons and Thaddeus Lowe. Four decades before Kitty Hawk and five decades before World War I, a few brave men went thousands of feet above enemy lines, hanging from a silk balloon, to spy out Confederate forces. Artillery shells burst around them, generals dismissed them, storms sent them careening, but the Balloon Corps played its part in American history, even if that history has gone untold for too long. Now read their heroic true story.

Nightmare Plagues (series)
Bearport, 2011.

> 1. ***Bubonic Plague: The Black Death!*** By Stephen Person.
> 2. ***The Flu of 1918: Millions Dead Worldwide!*** By Jessica Rudolph.
> 3. ***Malaria: Super Killer!*** By Stephen Person.
> 4. ***Smallpox: Is It Over?*** By Adam Reingold.
> 5. ***Tuberculosis: The White Plague!*** By Miriam Aronin.
> 6. ***Typhoid Fever: Dirty Food, Dirty Water!*** By William Caper.

HI/LO; SCIENCE Of all the things that have hunted man throughout the ages, the most terrifying have been invisible—not because they lurk in shadows, but because they are too small to see!

Poop Happened! A History of the World from the Bottom Up
By Sarah Albee. Illustrated by Robert Leighton. Walker, 2010.

HISTORY; HUMOR If this book teaches you anything, it's that if you try to ignore this . . . stuff . . . it doesn't go away, it just keeps piling up!

They Called Themselves the K.K.K.: The Birth of an American Terrorist Group
By Susan Campbell Bartoletti. Houghton Mifflin, 2010.

HISTORY We sometimes wish we could brush some of our history under the rug and try to forget it. We know we shouldn't, but sometimes our history hurts too much. The Ku Klux Klan is one of our darkest, most terrifying memories. Men draped in sheets riding through the night to terrorize the innocent is the stuff of horror films and nightmares. Do yourself a favor and shine a light on those memories with Susan Campbell Bartoletti's *They Called Themselves the K.K.K.*

True Tales of the Wild West (series)
By Jeff Savage. Enslow, 2012.

1. *American Cowboys*
2. *Daring Pony Express Riders*
3. *Fearless Scouts*
4. *Pioneering Women*
5. *Quick-Draw Gunfighters*
6. *Rugged Gold Miners*

HI/LO; HISTORY In one slim volume, *Quick-Draw Gun-fighters* has them all: the good and the bad, lawman and outlaw, those who died young and those who lived to tell the tales. Jesse James, Wild Bill Hickok, Wyatt Earp, Doc Holliday, Bat Masterson, and so many more. The men who colored the Wild West, and colored it red. How they lived and died—and why they lived and died—all at the point of a gun.

The Ultimate Survival Guide
By Mike Flynn. Illustrated by Mike Phillips. Macmillan, 2010.

ACTION, ADVENTURE, AND MYSTERY; SCIENCE Ever since the publication of Piven and Borgenicht's Worst-Case Scenario series, there has been a rash of survival books, most disappointingly tame and with little information about the great outdoors. *The Ultimate Survival Guide* is the real thing, a guide that talks about real-life survival situations from your backyard to the harshest environments on

Earth. Complete with activities like building a solar water purifier and a bit of British humor, this is the book for all those boys who were sorely disappointed by *The Dangerous Book for Boys*. Then move on to more real-life science on the edge with the rest of the series.

High School Nonfiction

Beyond Courage: The Untold Story of Jewish Resistance during the Holocaust
By Doreen Rappaport. Candlewick, 2012.

HISTORY The horror of the Holocaust can leave the impression that the Jews of Europe just waited to be slaughtered. But that isn't the whole story. All over Europe, Jews organized, helped one another escape the Nazis, made allies, and fought back. Often without help, often without hope, they fought so that the world would know they fought, in towns, ghettos, fields, forests, and even the death camps themselves.

Bloody Times: The Funeral of Abraham Lincoln and the Manhunt for Jefferson Davis
By James L. Swanson. Collins, 2011.

HISTORY; MILITARY When General Robert E. Lee surrendered to Ulysses S. Grant on April 9, 1865, the Union thought that the Civil War was over. Two men—Jefferson Davis, president of the Confederate States of America, and John Wilkes Booth, the soon-to-be assassin—did not agree. The war would not truly be over until the country buried Abraham Lincoln and hunted down Jefferson Davis.

Bulu: African Wonder Dog
By Dick Houston. Random House, 2010.

ANIMALS; BIOGRAPHY, AUTOBIOGRAPHY, AND MEMOIR; SCIENCE A cute little dog story on a boys and books list? Well, this cute little story is true, and this dog adopts warthogs and fights lions. This is more than a dog story—it is a safari into the wild African bush, with hippos, giraffes, crocodiles, and real-life adventure to spare.

Chasing Lincoln's Killer
By James L. Swanson. Scholastic, 2009.

HISTORY John Wilkes Booth originally planned to kidnap Abraham Lincoln and demand a Union surrender as ransom. But when the war ended before he could carry out his plan, he simply walked through all security, shot the president of the United States, and escaped while the audience at Ford's Theatre wondered if all the commotion was just part of the play. Thus started the greatest manhunt in American history, a twelve-day chase for the greatest traitor since Benedict Arnold. But there was so much more to the story: plots and subplots, coconspirators, other victims, and ultimately four bodies hanging from the gallows. Everyone knows about the scene in a theater box where the hero of the Civil War was assassinated; here, told in the words and the documents of the day, is the rest of the story.

Electrified Sheep: Glass-Eating Scientists, Nuking the Moon, and More Bizarre Experiments
By Alex Boese. Thomas Dunne Books, 2012.

SCIENCE Quick, what mad scientist first revived a shock victim using mouth-to-mouth resuscitation? And who was the victim? Answer: The scientist was Ben Franklin, and the victim was a chicken. And that's just one of the weird stories in this collection.

Fist Stick Knife Gun: A Personal History of Violence
By Geoffrey Canada. Adapted by Jamar Nicholas. Beacon Press, 2010.

BIOGRAPHY, AUTOBIOGRAPHY, AND MEMOIR; COMICS, MANGA, AND GRAPHIC LITERATURE "Possessing a gun feels like the ultimate form of protection. On the streets of a big American city, having this kind of personal protection may even seem to some to make sense. But it doesn't. I know from personal experience . . . In 1971, well before the explosion of handguns on the streets of New York City, I bought a handgun." This is an adaptation of what is becoming a classic work, done in comic form.

The Lost City of Z: A Tale of Deadly Obsession in the Amazon
By David Grann. Doubleday, 2009.

ACTION, ADVENTURE, AND MYSTERY; HISTORY; SCIENCE This nonfiction account covers a hundred years of fateful, and even fatal, expeditions into the heart of the Amazon region. It is part adventure tale, part horror story, part ecological treatise, all wrapped up in some amazing storytelling. This is Bill Bryson with teeth! It is a tropical *Into Thin Air*. Journalist David Grann follows in the footsteps of some of the greatest explorers ever into a land that even the great explorers could not conquer to try to solve a mystery as old as history in the New World: he goes in search of the golden city of El Dorado.

My Friend Dahmer

By Derf Backderf. Abrams ComicArts, 2012.

BIOGRAPHY, AUTOBIOGRAPHY, AND MEMOIR; COMICS, MANGA, AND GRAPHIC LITERATURE The formative years of one of the most notorious serial killers in American history are recounted here by someone who grew up with Jeffrey Dahmer.

No Dribbling the Squid: Octopush, Shin Kicking, Elephant Polo, and Other Oddball Sports

By Michael J. Rosen with Ben Kassoy. Andrews McMeel, 2009.

SPORTS Competitive spitting, shovel racing, backward bicycling, basketball on unicycles, and Octopush (underwater hockey)—there are some really strange sports out there, and they are all in this one little book, with plenty of pictures of all the zaniness. Two or three pages on each sport—complete with statistics, rules, and probably too many bad puns—make this a quick, fun read. No need to read it cover to cover; flip it open to any page and enjoy. (Hint: Kudu dung spitting on page 72.)

Signing Their Rights Away: The Fame and Misfortune of the Men Who Signed the United States Constitution

By Denise Kiernan and Joseph D'Agnese. Quirk Books, 2011.

BIOGRAPHY, AUTOBIOGRAPHY, AND MEMOIR; HISTORY Who needs (or wants) a textbook? Here in this little book is the history of not just the Constitution, but slavery, the Revolutionary War, a Supreme Court justice who was thrown in jail, and the little guy from the little state who cast the one vote that made America possible.

The Smart Aleck's Guide to American History

By Adam Selzer. Delacorte, 2009.

HISTORY Here is the cure for the common history book. This irreverent take on American history digs into such weighty issues as the place of stupid hats at major junctions of history, who was the most boring president we ever had, and why Americans have smelled so bad for so long. Read this alongside your real history textbook and you might get a few laughs and a little perspective.

Soldier Dogs: The Untold Story of America's Canine Heroes

By Maria Goodavage. Dutton, 2012.

ANIMALS; HISTORY; MILITARY A journalist takes us inside the lives of military dogs and their handlers, their selection, training, and acts of heroism with plenty of human (and canine) interest stories woven through. An especially unique view of the wars in Iraq and Afghanistan, this book makes a way of life few of us have ever imagined very real and personal.

Still I Rise: A Graphic History of African Americans
By Roland Laird with Taneshia Nash Laird. Illustrated by Elihu "Adofo" Bey. Sterling, 2009.

COMICS, MANGA, AND GRAPHIC LITERATURE; HISTORY A stunning, sweeping history told as much visually as in words, updated to include the historic election of Barack Obama.

Taxes, the Tea Party, and Those Revolting Rebels: A History in Comics of the American Revolution
By Stan Mack. Nantier, Beall, Minoustchine, 2012.

COMICS, MANGA, AND GRAPHIC LITERATURE; HISTORY; MILITARY Hey, maybe the people who decided that a bunch of backwater colonists could defeat the greatest army ever really were cartoon characters. Their stories seem far more real in this comic history than they ever did in a textbook.

The Warrior's Heart:
Becoming a Man of Compassion and Courage
By Eric Greitens. Houghton Mifflin, 2012.

BIOGRAPHY, AUTOBIOGRAPHY, AND MEMOIR; MILITARY "Many of the guys grew up in a culture where they'd inherited ideals about manhood from beer commercials and sit-coms. And whether the men they saw on TV were portrayed as overgrown and selfish boys, or as wimps and goofballs, the men who came to [Navy SEAL training] knew—even if they didn't articulate it—that there had to be more to being a man than that. They wanted to earn something, to pass through a test. They wanted to become strong and worthy."

Elementary Fiction

The Adventures of Ook and Gluk:
Kung-Fu Cavemen from the Future
By Dav Pilkey. Blue Sky Press, 2010.

COMICS, MANGA, AND GRAPHIC LITERATURE; HUMOR . . . and a barfing lizard saves the day! Dav Pilkey is well known for his groundbreaking series Captain Underpants. Ook and Gluk has the same humor but in a less identifiable setting, which might sit better with those parents who are uncomfortable with the idea of a principal in his underwear.

Aliens on Vacation

By Clete Barrett Smith. Illustrated by Christian Slade. Disney/Hyperion, 2011.

SCIENCE FICTION A mash-up of classic situational comedy and classic otherworldly science fiction, this is one for parents and boy to read together. What to read after Bruce Coville's *Aliens Ate My Homework*.

The Cartoon Chronicles of America (series)

By Stan Mack and Susan Champlin. Bloomsbury.

> 1. *Road to Revolution.* 2009.
> 2. *Fight for Freedom.* 2012.

COMICS, MANGA, AND GRAPHIC LITERATURE; HISTORICAL FICTION; MILITARY It's the Civil War, near the front lines, and everything about life on a southern plantation has been thrown into chaos. The slaves aren't free, but they aren't really slaves either. Proper southern women can no longer be proper southern women. You can't tell "us" from "them" because nobody knows who we are and who they are. Two children, one white and one black, who grew up together in the old world will have to find a way to make it in a whole new world in this comic book story.

Darth Vader and Son

By Jeffrey Brown. Chronicle Books, 2012.

COMICS, MANGA, AND GRAPHIC LITERATURE; SCIENCE FICTION "It is pointless to resist, my son. It's bedtime." There are things dads say and do that are so different when dad is Darth Vader. There are things Darth Vader does that mean so much more when he is a dad. Read this collection of comics featuring Darth and Luke with a Jedi you love.

Dragonbreath (series)

By Ursula Vernon. Dial.

> 1. *Dragonbreath.* 2009.
> 2. *Attack of the Ninja Frogs.* 2010.
> 3. *Curse of the Were-Wiener.* 2010.
> 4. *Lair of the Bat Monster.* 2011.
> 5. *No Such Thing as Ghosts.* 2011.
> 6. *Revenge of the Horned Bunnies.* 2012.
> 7. *When Fairies Go Bad.* 2012.
> 8. *Nightmare of the Iguana.* 2013.
> 9. *The Case of the Toxic Mutants.* 2013.

COMICS, MANGA, AND GRAPHIC LITERATURE; HUMOR Danny Dragonbreath, the fire-breathing-delayed dragon, faces down a freakish Frank in a cafeteria smackdown for the ages, takes the bus to Fairie Land and ancient Japan, battles jackalopes and ninja frogs, and generally does the whole scary/funny routine in this hybrid graphic/text series for the younger crowd.

Escape by Night: A Civil War Adventure
By Laurie Myers. Illustrated by Amy June Bates. Henry Holt, 2011.

CHRISTIAN FICTION; HISTORICAL FICTION; MILITARY Nine-year-old Tommy McKnight knows where to put his trust and loyalty: God, family, his beloved Georgia, and the Confederacy. But what will he do when being loyal to one makes him disloyal to another?

The Flying Beaver Brothers (series)
By Maxwell Eaton III. Knopf.

> 1. *The Flying Beaver Brothers and the Evil Penguin Plan.* 2012.
> 2. *The Flying Beaver Brothers and the Fishy Business.* 2012.
> 3. *The Flying Beaver Brothers and the Mud-Slinging Moles.* 2013.
> 4. *The Flying Beaver Brothers: Birds vs. Bunnies.* 2013.

ANIMALS; COMICS, MANGA, AND GRAPHIC LITERATURE; HUMOR Ace and Bub are surfing, aeronautical beavers who live on Beaver Island, an island entirely inhabited by beavers. Then it starts getting silly.

Fred Bowen Sports Stories (series)
By Fred Bowen. Peachtree.

> 1. *Soccer Team Upset.* 2009.
> 2. *Touchdown Trouble.* 2009.
> 3. *Dugout Rivals.* 2010.
> 4. *Hardcourt Comeback.* 2010.
> 5. *Throwing Heat.* 2010.
> 6. *Quarterback Season.* 2011.
> 7. *Real Hoops.* 2011.
> 8. *Go for the Goal!* 2012.
> 9. *Perfect Game.* 2013.

SPORTS *Quarterback Season* looks at all those moments that make a season, told convincingly in the voice of an eighth-grade quarterback, with all the excitement, disappointments, jealousy, and satisfaction of school sports. In *Throwing Heat*, Jack Lerner, a middle school flamethrower, is starting to compare his pitching speed with major leaguers—until he hits a new league where the hitters don't seem impressed. It is the story of a thrower faced with the daunting task of becoming a pitcher. *Touchdown Trouble* looks at that "uh-oh" moment in sports when everything that was sure becomes unsure, when everything is on the line. You will never see the moment coming, and when it happens, you won't believe you didn't see it coming. Fred Bowen is one of those sports journalists like Mike Lupica and Jon Feinstein who can write believably and engagingly for the young sports fan.

Ghost Buddy (series)
By Henry Winkler and Lin Oliver. Scholastic.

1. *Zero to Hero.* 2012.
2. *Mind If I Read Your Mind?* 2012.
3. *How to Scare the Pants Off Your Pets.* 2013.

GOTHIC HORROR, SUPERNATURAL, AND SUSPENSE; HUMOR Billy Broccoli's first friend in his new neighborhood calls him Billy-Boy, dances like a chicken, juggles breakfast cereal, wears suspenders—and he is going to teach Billy how to be cool. Oh, and he's been dead for ninety-nine years.

Grizzly Tales: Cautionary Tales for Lovers of Squeam (series)
By Jamie Rix. Orion.

1. *Nasty Little Beasts.* 2010.
2. *Gruesome Grown Ups.* 2010.
3. *The "ME!" Monsters.* 2010.
4. *Freaks of Nature.* 2010.
5. *Terror Time Toys.* 2010.
6. *Blubbers and Sicksters.* 2010.
7. *The Gnaughty Gnomes of "No!"* 2010.
8. *Superzeroes.* 2010.

GOTHIC HORROR, SUPERNATURAL, AND SUSPENSE Who doesn't like to see the mean, the nasty, and the selfish get their due? These creepy little tales of the inhabitants of the Hothell Darkness warn of the demonic retribution for those little children who don't clean their rooms, are mean to pets or little sisters, or start every sentence with "I want!" Ghastly and giggly, and just a little British, these kids' bedtime stories are a cross between Edgar Allen Poe and Roald Dahl.

The Haunting of Derek Stone (series)
By Tony Abbott. Scholastic, 2009.

1. *City of the Dead*
2. *Bayou Dogs*
3. *The Red House*
4. *The Ghost Road*

GOTHIC HORROR, SUPERNATURAL, AND SUSPENSE A bizarre confluence of two accidents opens a rift between the land of the living and the land of the dead, and they are coming for us!

The Imagination Station (series)
Tyndale House.

1. *Voyage with the Vikings.* By Marianne Hering and Paul McCusker. Illustrated by David Hohn. 2010.
2. *Attack at the Arena.* By Marianne Hering and Paul McCusker. Illustrated by David Hohn. 2010.
3. *Peril in the Palace.* By Marianne Hering and Paul McCusker. Illustrated by David Hohn. 2011.
4. *Revenge of the Red Knight.* By Marianne Hering and Paul McCusker. Illustrated by David Hohn. 2011.
5. *Showdown with the Shepherd.* By Marianne Hering and Brock Eastman. Illustrated by David Hohn. 2011.
6. *Problems in Plymouth.* By Marianne Hering and Marshal Younger. Illustrated by David Hohn. 2011.
7. *Secret of the Prince's Tomb.* By Marianne Hering and Marshal Younger. Illustrated by David Hohn. 2012.
8. *Battle for Cannibal Island.* By Marianne Hering and Wayne Thomas Batson. Illustrated by David Hohn. 2012.
9. *Escape to the Hiding Place.* By Marianne Hering and Marshal Younger. Illustrated by David Hohn. 2012.
10. *Challenge on the Hill of Fire.* By Marianne Hering and Nancy I. Sanders. Illustrated by David Hohn. 2012.

CHRISTIAN FICTION; FANTASY AND MAGICAL REALISM All the wonder and adventure of The Magic Tree House series, with a decidedly Christian bent. Patrick and Beth are young cousins who explore the world and all of time, and what it means to be good and faithful people while they are doing it.

Jack and Jill Went Up to Kill:
A Book of Zombie Nursery Rhymes

By Michael P. Spradlin. Illustrated by Jeff Weigel. Harper, 2011.

GOTHIC HORROR, SUPERNATURAL, AND SUSPENSE; HUMOR You never realize how many sheep there are in nursery rhymes until these most timid of creatures become the ravenous undead.

Lunch Lady (series)

By Jarrett J. Krosoczka. Knopf.

1. *Lunch Lady and the Cyborg Substitute.* 2009.
2. *Lunch Lady and the League of Librarians.* 2009.
3. *Lunch Lady and the Author Visit Vendetta.* 2009.
4. *Lunch Lady and the Summer Camp Shakedown.* 2010.
5. *Lunch Lady and the Bake Sale Bandit.* 2010.
6. *Lunch Lady and the Field Trip Fiasco.* 2011.
7. *Lunch Lady and the Mutant Mathletes.* 2012.
8. *Lunch Lady and the Picture Day Peril.* 2012.
9. *Lunch Lady and the Video Game Villain.* 2013.

COMICS, MANGA, AND GRAPHIC LITERATURE; HUMOR It's high adventure served up hot from the school cafeteria with villainy and triumph and lots of goofy gadgets. Just what to give kids who have read *Captain Underpants* twelve times.

The Sapphire Knight

By Michael Sullivan. Illustrated by Douglas Sirois. PublishingWorks, 2009.

FANTASY A young traveler sits beside a fire on an open heath and hears a most amazing tale from a broken and disfigured old man, a tale of sorcery and battle between the light of a great white castle and the dark green wood, between the White Lady and the Green Queen. Caught between two great powers, a young knight must discover truth and his own courage to defend that truth. But is it just an idle tale of a lying old man, or is it the true history of the Sapphire Knight?

Stone Rabbit (series)

By Erik Craddock. Random House.

1. *BC Mambo.* 2009.
2. *Pirate Palooza.* 2009.

3. *Deep-Space Disco.* 2009.
4. *Superhero Stampede.* 2010.
5. *Ninja Slice.* 2010.
6. *Night of the Living Dust Bunnies.* 2011.
7. *Dragon Boogie.* 2012.
8. *Robot Frenzy.* 2013.

ANIMALS; COMICS, MANGA, AND GRAPHIC LITERATURE; HUMOR The floppy-eared flunky with the worst luck in history—and prehistory, and posthistory apparently—takes us on wild ride after wild ride with galactic meanies, mad scientist cavemen, killer robots, deadly smoothies, game-saving barbecue sauce, a molasses-breathing dragon, and so much more.

Topps League Stories (series) (Baseball)
By Kurtis Scaletta. Amulet.

1. *Jinxed! Illustrated by Eric Wight.* 2012.
2. *Steal That Base! Illustrated by Eric Wight.* 2012.
3. *Zip It! Illustrated by Eric Wight.* 2012.
4. *The 823rd Hit. Illustrated by Eric Wight.* 2012.
5. *You're Out! Illustrated by Ethen Beavers.* 2013.
6. *Batter Up! Illustrated by Ethen Beavers.* 2013.

SPORTS Oh, the minor leagues! Goofy players, strange superstitions, rodents, dugout gags, and desperate young players who will do anything to end a slump. A very funny sports series for the young fan.

Underworlds (series)
By Tony Abbott. Illustrated by Antonio Javier Caparo. Scholastic.

1. *The Battle Begins.* 2011.
2. *When Monsters Escape.* 2012.
3. *Revenge of the Scorpion King.* 2012.
4. *The Ice Dragon.* 2012.

FANTASY AND MAGICAL REALISM Owen Brown is unaware of all the underworlds of mythology—until they find a hole in our world where his best friend is standing. Suddenly, Dana is missing and Owen is on a quest to drag her back from the land of the dead. For all those aspiring Rick Riordan readers out there, here is where your quest begins.

Middle School Fiction

Archvillain (series)

By Barry Lyga. Scholastic.

> *1. Archvillain.* 2010.
> *2. The Mad Mask.* 2012.
> *3. Yesterday Again.* 2013.

HUMOR; SCIENCE FICTION Hero stories are usually told from the point of view of, well, the hero. But what if you were looking over the shoulder of "the bad guy"? Barry Lyga gives us a very funny superhero story for all those who thought Lex Luther was just misunderstood.

Bad Island

By Doug TenNapel. Graphix, 2011.

COMICS, MANGA, AND GRAPHIC LITERATURE; SCIENCE FICTION A sci-fi riff on Jules Verne's *The Mysterious Island?* In comic book form? With flying robots? That's just not fair.

The Berinfell Prophecies (series)

By Wayne Thomas Batson and Christopher Hopper. Thomas Nelson.

> *1. Curse of the Spider King.* 2009.
> *2. Venom and Song.* 2010.
> *3. The Tide of Unmaking.* 2012.

CHRISTIAN FICTION; FANTASY The entire race of elves was all but wiped out by a vicious assault. Their hopes hang on a bloodline kept safe in the human world for eight hundred years, on seven children with powers they don't even know they have, and the words of their God as a shield against their enemies.

Big Nate (series)

By Lincoln Peirce. Harper.

> *1. Big Nate: In a Class by Himself.* 2010.
> *2. Big Nate Strikes Again.* 2010.
> *3. Big Nate on a Roll.* 2011.
> *4. Big Nate Goes for Broke.* 2012.
> *5. Big Nate: What Could Possibly Go Wrong?* 2012.
> *6. Big Nate: Here Goes Nothing.* 2012.
> *7. Big Nate Flips Out.* 2013.

COMICS, MANGA, AND GRAPHIC LITERATURE; HUMOR Getting a detention slip from a teacher who doesn't even bother to write your name, just "Kid with the weird hair"? That's a bad day! Wet stains on your gym shorts, 148 servings of green beans, and having your teacher find your list of nicknames for her—that's a world record bad day. This series combines texts and comics to make one very funny mix.

The Brotherband Chronicles (series)
By John Flanagan. Philomel.

1. *The Outcasts.* 2011.
2. *The Invaders.* 2012.
3. *The Hunters.* 2012.

FANTASY AND MAGICAL REALISM The Ranger's Apprentice series is dead; long live the Brotherband Chronicles! Flanagan doesn't wander far from the formula that made his earlier series such a joy: heroism, courage, character, and fast-paced action. There are new characters and new challenges in the same world, and the new hero, Hal, will gain loyal followers from the outset.

Cal Ripken Jr.'s All-Stars (series)
By Cal Ripken Jr. with Kevin Cowherd. Disney/Hyperion.

1. *Hothead.* 2011.
2. *Super-Sized Slugger.* 2012.
3. *Wild Pitch.* 2013.

SPORTS Connor Sullivan has it all for the Orioles Babe Ruth League Baseball team: he can field, throw, run, hit, and hit for power. All of which does him no good if he can't keep his temper and keep himself from being kicked off the field, maybe for good. Cody Parker is thrilled to have landed on his new baseball team, and most of the Orioles are thrilled to have their new third baseman and fifth-hitting slugger. Who isn't thrilled? How about the Oriole's old third baseman and fifth-hitting slugger? A baseball legend brings both a ton of knowledge and great love for the game to this series.

Cardboard
By Doug TenNapel. Graphix, 2012.

COMICS, MANGA, AND GRAPHIC LITERATURE; GOTHIC HORROR, SUPERNATURAL, AND SUSPENSE It's Pinocchio! Well, with self-replicating monsters bent on destroying the world and replacing it with their own demonic cardboard reality. Bwahahaha!!!

Chomp
By Carl Hiaasen. Knopf, 2012.

ANIMALS; HUMOR Alligators, pythons, monkeys, iguanas, bats, mosquitoes, television reality show stars—there is no end of things that will bite you in the Florida Everglades.

The Creature from the Seventh Grade: Boy or Beast?
By Bob Balaban. Illustrated by Andy Rash. Viking, 2012.

HUMOR; SCIENCE FICTION "Suddenly I can feel my teeth getting longer and sharper. My neck grows longer, too. And skinnier. I stare, transfixed, at my fingers as each of my hands morphs into a claw with three sharp talons. My toenails burst through my sneakers. I cross my legs and try to hide my lower extremities under my desk. It's my nightmare come true: I, Charles Elmer Drinkwater, am turning into the Creature from the Black Lagoon." This is the first in a series.

Crosswire
By Dotti Enderle. Calkins Creek, 2010.

HISTORICAL FICTION A teenage boy experiences the danger and struggle of the taming of the Texas plains when his family's ranch is threatened by violent gangs who cut fences, kill livestock, and threaten ranchers in a war to keep the plains open. In a time and place where the law doesn't really exist, it is a man, his gun, and the courage to use it that stands between life and death—but is Jesse really ready to stand up and be that man?

Dead End in Norvelt
By Jack Gantos. Farrar, Straus and Giroux, 2011.

HUMOR What kid hasn't dreamed of rewriting their own life? But when the author of the Joey Pigza books does it, well, fiction really is stranger—and funnier—than truth.

Erebos
By Ursula Poznanski. Translated by Judith Pattinson. Annick Press, 2012.

SCIENCE FICTION Any real gamer will tell you, "It isn't just a game." And it isn't; it knows things. It can converse with you. It can order you to do things. And somehow, you just can't say no. It isn't just a game—this game is murder.

Game Changers (series)
By Mike Lupica. Scholastic.

1. *Game Changers.* 2012. (Football)
2. *Play Makers.* 2013. (Basketball)

SPORTS Everyone thinks the quarterback has to be a leader on a football team. But does a leader have to be a quarterback? And does being a quarterback make you a leader? Mike Lupica is back with his best book since *Heat*, doing what he does best, reminding all of us why we love the game.

The Ghost of Graylock
By Dan Poblocki. Scholastic, 2012.

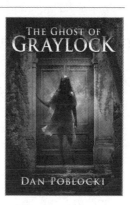

GOTHIC HORROR, SUPERNATURAL, AND SUSPENSE
Abandoned buildings are spooky. Abandoned buildings in the woods are creepier. Put it in the mountains, on an island in the middle of a lake, and you have the perfect setting for a horror story. Add to that the fact that the abandoned building was an insane asylum, with a special ward for troubled teenagers who ended up dead at an alarming rate, and stories are bound to circulate. Nobody would be crazy enough to go poking around in there . . . would they?

Ghostopolis
By Doug TenNapel. Graphix, 2010.

COMICS, MANGA, AND GRAPHIC LITERATURE; FANTASY AND MAGICAL REALISM
This riff on *The Wizard of Oz* supercharges everything: The wizard isn't some benign old man behind a curtain, he is a mighty sorcerer who is not about to give up control of his kingdom. There is no Glenda the good witch, but a twelve-foot black man with a Jesus complex. No flying monkeys, just demonic man-sized bugs. And Toto is a skeleton horse. No, Garth, you aren't in Kansas anymore; this is the afterlife!

The Heroes of Olympus (series)
By Rick Riordan. Disney/Hyperion.

  1. *The Lost Hero.* 2010.
  2. *The Son of Neptune.* 2011.
  3. *The Mark of Athena.* 2012.
  4. *The Demigod Diaries.* 2012.

FANTASY AND MAGICAL REALISM Riordan returns to his world of classical mythology meets modern times, and all the magic is still there. Percy Jackson is gone (one of the central plot elements), making room for new heroes and a new look at Camp Half Blood, a new way of seeing the gods, and all new terrors from the netherworld.

I Funny: A Middle School Story

By James Patterson and Chris Grabenstein. Illustrated by Laura Park. Little, Brown, 2012.

HUMOR Stand-up comedian? Hey, Jamie Grimm would be happy just to stand up! But seriously folks, what did this kid in a wheelchair do to be sentenced to three years in a state institution: middle school? Well, any experience you can walk away from . . . oh, sorry. So how do you survive zombies, bullies, teachers, girls, and other scary creatures? Yuck it up and leave 'em laughing.

Island of Thieves

By Josh Lacey. Houghton Mifflin, 2012.

ACTION, ADVENTURE, AND MYSTERY Hunting for lost Spanish gold promises danger and fortune, but there is more danger and more fortune in play than troublemaking Tom Trelawney could ever dream of when he follows his uncle to Peru, looking for the lost Island of Thieves.

Jason Steed (series)

By Mark A. Cooper. Sourcebooks Jabberwocky.

1. *Fledgling.* 2010.
2. *Revenge.* 2012.

ACTION, ADVENTURE, AND MYSTERY It's nonstop spy action with a 12-year-old multiple-black-belt secret agent. If your son was enamored by Anthony Horowitz's Alex Rider series, well, Jason Steed makes Alex Rider look like a wimp.

Joshua Dread

By Lee Bacon. Delacorte, 2012.

SCIENCE FICTION It's a dangerous world, full of supervillains terrorizing the world. Middle schooler Joshua Dread would take comfort in the fact that there are superheroes too, like Captain Justice, if his parents weren't making him dinner, helping him with his homework, and terrorizing the world.

The Kane Chronicles (series)

By Rick Riordan. Disney/Hyperion.

1. *The Red Pyramid.* 2010.
2. *The Throne of Fire.* 2011.
3. *The Serpent's Shadow.* 2012.

4. *The Kane Chronicles Survival Guide.* By Mary-Jane Knight. Illustrated by Antonio Caparo, Philip Chidlow, and Artful Doodlers. 2012.

FANTASY AND MAGICAL REALISM The ancient gods and goddesses are real! No, not the Greek gods and goddesses; that was Rick Riordan's other series. And two kids are descended from the gods. No, they aren't the direct children of gods, that's Rick Riordan's other series too. There's a war brewing, and the descendants of the gods must play their part. Yeah, I know, that was also in the other series, but any kid who loved Percy Jackson (and what kid didn't?) will line up for the Kane Chronicles.

The Last Musketeer
By Stuart Gibbs. Harper, 2011.

FANTASY AND MAGICAL REALISM Want a little swashbuckling in your reading? Why not go back to a real original, with a modern twist? This retelling of the classic *The Three Musketeers* by Alexander Dumas brings a little magic into the story to connect that world with modern times.

Lucky: Maris, Mantle, and My Best Summer Ever
By Wes Tooke. Simon and Schuster, 2010.

SPORTS Baseball players are real people. Even big leaguers. Even New York Yankees. Even baseball legends chasing one of the greatest records in all of sports are real guys. Louis "Lucky" May could not have been luckier when he gets a chance to know the real Mickey Mantle and Roger Maris as they went after the great Babe Ruth's single-season home-run record.

A Monster Calls
By Patrick Ness. Candlewick, 2011.

GOTHIC HORROR, SUPERNATURAL, AND SUSPENSE This book reminds us of the great secret of gothic literature: the dark isn't necessarily evil; it is something far more frightening—it is the unknown. We aren't afraid of what lurks in the dark, we are afraid of the dark itself.

Mush! Sled Dogs with Issues
By Glenn Eichler and Joe Infurnari. First Second, 2011.

ANIMALS; COMICS, MANGA, AND GRAPHIC LITERATURE; HUMOR Harebrained philosopher, reluctant hero, conniving backstabber, blue-blood snob—hey, dogs are people too!

No Place like Holmes (series)
By Jason Lethcoe. Thomas Nelson, 2011.

1. *No Place like Holmes*
2. *The Future Door*

CHRISTIAN FICTION; MYSTERY Griffin Sharpe wants to be a detective in the mold of his hero, Sherlock Holmes, and he has the keenest intellect to do it, though he is only a boy. His uncle wants to be a very different kind of detective, one that uses science and technology to peer into truth. The message is clear: neither approach alone is as strong as they are together. Griffin's comfortable and warm faith fits in well: intellect is not enough without a little divine strength and guidance.

On the Day I Died: Stories from the Grave
By Candice Fleming. Schwartz and Wade, 2012.

GOTHIC HORROR, SUPERNATURAL, AND SUSPENSE Everybody loves ghost stories, but what if the ghosts themselves were telling the stories?

Pinch Hit
By Tim Green. Harper, 2012.

SPORTS It's *The Prince and the Pauper*, with diving stabs of line drives and towering home runs. And modern American royalty: movie stars!

Planet Tad
By Tim Carvell. Illustrated by Doug Holgate. Harper, 2012.

HUMOR March 29: "My little sister Sophie's pretty upset—she was named for our great-aunt Sophie. She came into my room tonight and said, 'Where do you think Aunt Sophie went?' And I gave her the same answer my parents gave me when our golden retriever died. Great-Aunt Sophie was taken to a farm where she gets to spend all day chasing rabbits and playing with other great-aunts. That seemed to make her happy."

Playing for Keeps
By Steven Sandor. Lorimer, 2012.

HI/LO; SPORTS "A win is good. You know how people call soccer 'The Beautiful Game'? Well, the person who came up with that saying is dumb . . . sometimes you win ugly . . . You know what they call a team that wins games like that twenty times a year? Champions, that's what!"

The Ring of Solomon: A Bartimaeus Novel

By Jonathan Stroud. Disney/Hyperion, 2010.

FANTASY AND MAGICAL REALISM Everyone's favorite sarcastic djinni is back and in fine form, if he does say so himself. Powerful magic will be summoned, and powerful magicians will be eaten, in this fantasy follow-up to the Bartimaeus Trilogy.

Son of Angels, Jonah Stone (series)

By Jerel Law. Thomas Nelson.

1. *Spirit Fighter.* 2011.
2. *Fire Prophet.* 2012.
3. *Shadow Chaser.* 2013.

CHRISTIAN FICTION; GOTHIC HORROR, SUPERNATURAL, AND SUSPENSE Gird yourself in the armor of God; you're going to need it. When the grandson of a fallen angel comes face to face with all the forces of Hell on Earth, a flaming sword might come in very handy.

Storm Runners (series)

By Roland Smith. Scholastic.

1. *Storm Runners.* 2011.
2. *The Surge.* 2011.
3. *Eruption.* 2012.

ACTION, ADVENTURE, AND MYSTERY The "MD" on the truck doesn't stand for medical doctor, but for "Masters of Disaster," two guys and one teen who live on the road driving toward storms, fires, volcanoes, and all kinds of situations everyone else is fleeing from. What does growing up the son of a disaster recovery expert do for you? For Chase Masters, it makes you the one guy everybody can count on no matter what comes at you—and believe me, it is all coming at you.

The Talent Show

By Dan Gutman. Simon and Schuster, 2010.

HUMOR Which do you think will cause more chaos: a tornado, or a school full of kids with a stage, a microphone, and a desire to stick it to The Man? This town will never be the same, twice!

Take Me to the River

By Will Hobbs. Harper, 2011.

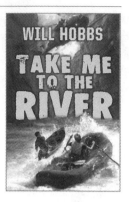

ACTION, ADVENTURE, AND MYSTERY Will Hobbs means adventure. Name the outdoor thrill ride, and Hobbs has written it, usually with layer upon layer of added dangers and complications. So when Dylan Sands sets off for a river adventure on the Rio Grande, well, you know the water will be wilder than he expects. But who would guess he would end up in the middle of a hurricane and an international manhunt? Anyone who has ever read Will Hobbs, that's who.

Tales from Lovecraft Middle School (series)

By Charles Gilman. Illustrated by Eugene Smith. Quirk Books.

1. *Professor Gargoyle.* 2012.
2. *The Slither Sisters.* 2013.
3. *Teacher's Pest.* 2013.

GOTHIC HORROR, SUPERNATURAL, AND SUSPENSE Well, they always said middle school was hell . . .

The Thin Executioner

By Darren Shan. Little, Brown, 2010.

GOTHIC HORROR, SUPERNATURAL, AND SUSPENSE From the author of The Saga of Darren Shan and Demonata series comes a . . . what? Gothic horror? Dark fantasy? Or a religious allegory in the mold of Pilgrim's Progress? Forget the labels and get lost in the quest of Jebel Rum to find the fiery mountain home of a terrible God, all in search of the honor and glory that is due a hero. What he finds instead is the kind of strength of which heroes are made.

Titanic (series)

By Gordon Korman. Scholastic, 2011.

1. *Unsinkable*
2. *Collision Course*
3. *S.O.S.*

HISTORICAL FICTION Thousands of deaths is a disaster, but it can seem unreal, especially a hundred years later. Korman does a masterful job of bringing the tragedy of the Titanic down to real life for a handful of kids, whose different backgrounds mean vastly different experiences when the great ship goes down. With all due respect to James Cameron, this is a whole lot more gritty and real than the movie, with a guest appearance by Jack the Ripper just to spice things up.

The Underdogs
By Mike Lupica. Philomel, 2011.

SPORTS A feel-good story with tons of football action from the dean of juvenile sports fiction. Something for the guys to read until *SportsCenter* comes on. With a kick-butt girl player too.

Ungifted
By Gordon Korman. Balzer and Bray, 2012.

HUMOR What does it mean to be gifted? Do you have to be smarter than the rest? Better at science and math? More effective with the English language? Know robotics and engineering? Be headed for a top-level college? Yes! And Donovan Curtis is none of those things. He is a wisecracking, troublemaking, C– on his best day kind of student. Let all those geniuses figure out what he is doing with them in the most advanced school for gifted children in the state.

Unstoppable
By Tim Green with Barbara Lalicki. Harper, 2012.

SPORTS Defensive linemen? Heck, they are nothing compared to what Harrison has had to deal with, and he has the bruises to show for it. Maybe that is what makes him so thrilled to throw his body into tacklers, and carry tacklers downfield on his back. After being beaten and kicked around as a foster kid, he can handle anything . . . until the worst of anything hits him from out of the blue.

Warriors in the Crossfire
By Nancy Bo Flood. Front Street, 2010.

HISTORICAL FICTION; MILITARY This is the seldom-told story of native peoples caught in the crossfire of World War II in the Pacific. The people of Saipan Island huddle between the occupying Japanese, who vow death to all rather than surrender, and the Americans who are said to be so vicious they eat children. Who do you fight for? Who do you fear most? And does it take more courage to fight or to survive?

Wild Rescue (series)
By J. Burchett and S. Vogler. Illustrated by Diane Le Feyer. Stone Arch, 2012.

1. *Poacher Panic*
2. *Earthquake Escape*
3. *Rainforest Rescue*
4. *Polar Meltdown*
5. *Safari Survival*
6. *Ocean S.O.S.*

7. *Avalanche Alert*
8. *Desert Danger*

ACTION, ADVENTURE, AND MYSTERY; ANIMALS; HI/LO What could be better than being a 12-year-old secret agent in defense of the most endangered animals on the planet?

Woods Runner
By Gary Paulsen. Wendy Lamb, 2010.

HISTORICAL FICTION; MILITARY If your first thought was Johnny Tremain, try this instead. Gary Paulsen's true strength may not be action-adventure but historical fiction. This fast-moving tale from the Revolutionary War encompasses not just the cities but the frontier, which is often lost in history. Short passages of historical fact are woven in with the narrative, making it read like both history and compelling story. This is one of Paulsen's best. When he's done reading this one, give him Paulsen's earlier work, *The Rifle*.

High School Fiction

American Vampire
By Scott Snyder and Rafael Albuquerque. Vertigo, 2010–. (Graphic series)

COMICS, MANGA, AND GRAPHIC LITERATURE; GOTHIC HORROR, SUPERNATURAL, AND SUSPENSE "Here's what vampires shouldn't be: pallid detectives who drink Bloody Marys and only work at night; lovelorn southern gentlemen; anorexic teenage girls; boy-toys with big dewy eyes. What should they be? Killers, honey. Stone killers . . ." (from the intro to volume 1 by Stephen King). Here is the antidote for all those guys who have had just too much *Twilight* waved in their faces.

Amped
By Daniel H. Wilson. Doubleday, 2012.

SCIENCE FICTION The problem with becoming more than human is that it somehow makes everyone else less than human, and they aren't going to like it. Expect trouble when you get amped.

Angry Young Man
By Chris Lynch. Simon and Schuster, 2011.

ACTION, ADVENTURE, AND MYSTERY Chris Lynch gets right to the ideals that get left out of too many teen books: honor, responsibility, loyalty—all the things that aspiring young men so often need to explore. Alexander is different, and that is fine with him. After all, "normal" is mean, brutal, heartless, and cruel. But when he finally sees a chance to stop fuming and actually do something to change the world, does he know any way to do it other than becoming the things he despises?

The Apprenticeship of Victor Frankenstein (series)

By Kenneth Oppel. Simon and Schuster.

1. ***This Dark Endeavor.*** 2011.
2. ***Such Wicked Intent.*** 2012.

GOTHIC HORROR, SUPERNATURAL, AND SUSPENSE The great men—powerful men, even terrible men—don't just appear on the pages of history. Even monsters come from somewhere. Even Frankenstein was a boy once . . .

The Ascendance Trilogy (series)

By Jennifer A. Nielsen. Scholastic.

1. ***The False Prince.*** 2012.
2. ***The Runaway King.*** 2013.

FANTASY AND MAGICAL REALISM A kingdom on the brink of civil war, facing enemies within and without its borders, torn by the ambitions of great men. The kingdom needs its lost prince, and one nobleman aims to give the kingdom what it needs, even if he has to make the prince from nothing. Enter Sage, an orphan boy and a thief, who lives for himself, destitute but free. Will he be his own man, the puppet of a powerful schemer, or the prince his kingdom needs him to be? And must he be just one?

The Assault

By Brian Faulkner. Recon Team Angel series, book 1. Random House, 2012.

MILITARY; SCIENCE FICTION An alien war in the classic science fiction tradition: the human race is striking back, into the heart of the enemy's homeland, but the only humans who can pull it off are an elite squad of teenage soldiers. And the alien homeland is right here on Earth.

Au Revoir, Crazy European Chick

By Joe Schreiber. Houghton Mifflin, 2011.

ACTION, ADVENTURE, AND MYSTERY This one starts off like a typical teen-angst novel, but soon enough, Perry Stormaire has a lot more to worry about than bullies, high school, and cheerleaders. It's a nonstop, action-adventure shoot-'em-up with fast cars and hip bars, explosions and helicopters . . . The sequel is *Perry's Killer Playlist* (Houghton Mifflin, 2012).

The Berlin Boxing Club

By Robert Sharenow. HarperTeen, 2011.

HISTORICAL FICTION; SPORTS Any real sports fan will tell you, sports are life. So for a Jewish boy growing up in Nazi Germany, nothing is more natural than strapping on the gloves and getting into the ring. Punishing, sure, but in and out of the ring, Karl Stern is fighting for his life.

Blacksad

By Juan Díaz Canales and Juanjo Guarnido. Dark Horse, 2010.

ACTION, ADVENTURE, AND MYSTERY; COMICS, MANGA, AND GRAPHIC LITERATURE It's comics noir, dark and rich and edgy and smart. The characters have their human weaknesses, but their animal nature shows in their faces. Life in the big city really is a jungle, and the bad guys would do well to fear the big black cat.

Boy21

By Matthew Quick. Little, Brown, 2012.

ACTION, ADVENTURE, AND MYSTERY; SPORTS Everybody has secrets. Nobody talks. So when Boy21, the greatest basketball prospect since Kobe Bryant, shows up in a mob-infested New Jersey slum, claiming to be from outer space, all you really know for sure is that the truth is more explosive than the lies.

Brody's Ghost

By Mark Crilley. Dark Horse, 2010–. (Manga)

COMICS, MANGA, AND GRAPHIC LITERATURE; GOTHIC HORROR, SUPERNATURAL, AND SUSPENSE From the streets of a futuristic city rises a new hero. Brody has to let go of everything to gain the one thing he needs, a destiny. Aided by a ghost assigned a "life task" before she can move on to the afterlife, and a spirit that is himself haunted by a distant failure, Brody must strike a blow for the good against a serial killer who preys on the innocent.

Bruiser

By Neal Shusterman. HarperTeen, 2010.

FANTASY AND MAGICAL REALISM Gift? Or curse? To be able to take the pain from those you love; to be unable not to take the pain of those you love. Pain is part of what makes us human. What does it make us if someone takes our pain away? And what does it make that person?

Cage of Eden

By Yoshinobu Yamada. Translated by Mari Morimoto. Kodansha Comics, 2011–. (Manga)

COMICS, MANGA, AND GRAPHIC LITERATURE High school survivors of a plane wreck find themselves stranded on an island that never existed, with creatures that shouldn't exist, and controlled by rules that no longer exist. It's *Lord of the Flies* meets *The Mysterious Island* in a thrilling manga.

Calico Joe

By John Grisham. Doubleday, 2012.

SPORTS A young phenom, on the greatest tear that any rookie has ever gone on in Major League Baseball history, digs in against an embittered pitcher spiraling toward an ugly end to his career. What happens next would reverberate for thirty years. Oh, and the sound of breaking bones would be heard by fifty thousand fans.

Chew (series)

By John Layman and Rob Guillory. Image Comics.

1. *Taster's Choice.* 2009.
2. *International Flavor.* 2010.
3. *Just Desserts.* 2010.
4. *Flambé.* 2011.
5. *Major League Chew.* 2012.
6. *Space Cakes.* 2013.

ACTION, ADVENTURE, AND MYSTERY; COMICS, MANGA, AND GRAPHIC LITERATURE Tony Chu is a psychic who gets his readings by tasting things. That gets a bit gross when he becomes a homicide detective. You do the math. This series is, well, unique.

The Coldest City

By Antony Johnston. Illustrated by Sam Hart. Oni Press, 2012.

ACTION, ADVENTURE, AND MYSTERY; COMICS, MANGA, AND GRAPHIC LITERATURE; HISTORICAL FICTION The already dangerous world of international spies in the shadow of the Berlin Wall is teetering on chaos as the wall teeters on the verge of collapse. It is 1989, and all the secrets they have fought to keep are about to come out. In the scramble to "clean house," you may not know who the traitor is until there is only one left standing.

Crater: A Helium-3 Novel

By Homer Hickam. Thomas Nelson, 2012.

CHRISTIAN FICTION; SCIENCE FICTION Travel into space isn't going to be glamorous, zipping among the pretty stars. It will be hard men and women leading a hardscrabble life exploiting the mineral wealth of the moon for the wealthy and powerful in an unimaginably deadly environment. Out of this bleak future steps one young man, honest, sincere, naive of course, but devoted and, when necessary, fearless. The perfect tool for a powerful man bent on furthering his own ends.

Crazy Dangerous

By Andrew Klavan. Thomas Nelson, 2012.

CHRISTIAN FICTION; GOTHIC HORROR, SUPERNATURAL, AND SUSPENSE Do right. Fear nothing. Great advice, unless you are Sam Hopkins, whose world is about to spiral into a nightmare of sadistic thugs, conspiracies, and murder, where the only tie to the truth is a crazy girl who hears demons whispering and sees visions of horrors to come. And somewhere out there, a dark figure is pulling all the strings. It is Stephen King with a hauntingly believable teen boy's voice.

Croak (series)

By Gina Damico. Graphia, 2012.

1. *Croak*
2. *Scorch*

GOTHIC HORROR, SUPERNATURAL, AND SUSPENSE What do you do with a teenager who is violent, foul mouthed, and out of control? Put her in charge of death. Yeah, that oughtta work. For all those kids who loved Harry Potter then cooled a bit, Croak follows the Harry Potter format, just from a gothic angle rather than a fantasy one.

Dawn Land

By Joseph Bruchac. Adapted and illustrated by Will Davis. First Second, 2010.

COMICS, MANGA, AND GRAPHIC LITERATURE A sweeping epic by the greatest living Native American storyteller, retold brilliantly as a graphic novel with very few words. A journey, both physical and spiritual, to challenge the deep terrors that stalked the footsteps of ancient man for the future of the world. Mesmerizing.

Days of Little Texas

By R. A. Nelson. Knopf, 2009.

CHRISTIAN FICTION; GOTHIC HORROR, SUPERNATURAL, AND SUSPENSE The story of a young teen celebrity preacher takes a decidedly horrific twist. Christians may talk a lot about the devil, but wait until they come face to face with him!

Eleven Eleven

By Paul Dowswell. Bloomsbury, 2012.

HISTORICAL FICTION; MILITARY November 11, 1918, 5 a.m. Old men, who get to decide these things, decide that World War I, "The Great War," would end in six hours. The eleventh hour of the eleventh day of the eleventh month; it had a nice sound to it. It gave the old men time to tell everyone and make sure everyone was on board. It also gave young men six hours to die.

Failstate

By John W. Otte. Marcher Lord, 2012.

CHRISTIAN FICTION; SCIENCE FICTION It had to happen: a reality show to pick the next teen superhero! One caped contestant gets voted off every week, and Rob "Failstate" Laughlin knows his days are numbered. He isn't the superhuman, shiny, photogenic hero America expects. But the darkness he hides behind grunge clothes and a Halloween mask drives him like no other. He fights for redemption, propelled by a painful past and a desperate faith, in a way that the others may not understand. A rare Christian-centered approach to the classic superhero story.

Flip

By Martyn Bedford. Wendy Lamb, 2011.

FANTASY AND MAGICAL REALISM Many teens dream of living someone else's life—if they got to choose who and when, of course. But if you had to live someone else's life? What if you woke up with your mind and someone else's body, someone else's life? What does it really mean to be "you"? What does it mean to be nobody at all?

Galactic Football League (series)

By Scott Sigler. Diversion Books.

1. ***The Rookie.*** 2009.
2. ***The Starter.*** 2010.

3. *The All-Pro.* 2011.
4. *The MVP.* 2012.

SCIENCE FICTION; SPORTS Six-hundred-pound armored alien monsters as linemen, gorilla beasts at linebacker, scuttling bug creatures at receiver and defensive back, and a quarterback from some backwater human world just trying not to get his head ripped off on every play—that's the world of the Galactic Football League in this sci-fi/sports mash-up.

Gil Marsh

By A. C. E. Bauer. Random House, 2012.

SPORTS All heroes die. What makes them heroes is that their stories don't die. This retelling of Gilgamesh may be the first truly heroic tale you run into all year.

The Griff

By Christopher Moore and Ian Corson with Jennyson Rosero. William Morrow, 2011.

COMICS, MANGA, AND GRAPHIC LITERATURE; SCIENCE FICTION It's Jurassic Park, falling from the sky! In this graphic novel of alien invasion, the little green men are huge green dragon creatures, and the ETs aren't being cuddled by a cute little 6-year-old Drew Barrymore. The heroine is the Game Goddess, and who better to fight alien invaders than the woman who designed the video games where they, well, you know, fight alien invaders?

Guilty

By Norah McClintock. Orca, 2012.

ACTION, ADVENTURE, AND MYSTERY; HI/LO Two teens, their lives devastated by the adults in their lives. Her father killed his mother . . . twice. His father sent her father to prison, and when he got out, took him away again by killing him. In the shattering aftermath, there are few parents left, and precious little comfort, but enough guilt for everyone.

Habibi

By Craig Thompson. Pantheon, 2011.

COMICS, MANGA, AND GRAPHIC LITERATURE Epic. Mystic. Mythic. Powerful visual storytelling with no holds barred. Dodola and Zam are buffeted and abused. Cultures, races, even epochs collide and explode the world around them. In a world where the "other" is so feared and misunderstood, there is no more human way to see behind the veil of the Muslim world than to see two desperate people holding on to all they have left, Habibi, "my beloved."

The Hunt (series)

By Andrew Fukuda. St. Martin's Griffin.

1. **The Hunt.** 2012.
2. **The Prey.** 2013.

GOTHIC HORROR, SUPERNATURAL, AND SUSPENSE There are vampires lurking amid the hordes of humans . . . no, wait! It's the other way around! If one is fright ening, the other is terrifying. One slip, one human emotion, and you are doomed. In such a world, can you really be human at all?

Ikigami: The Ultimate Limit

By Motoro Mase. VIZ Media, 2009–. (Manga)

COMICS, MANGA, AND GRAPHIC LITERATURE For all dys-topia fans, here is a society that teaches the value of life, by randomly taking the lives of its young adults. If you were told you had twenty-four hours to live, what would you do? No simple answers here; one of the most innovative man-gas in recent years.

The Klaatu Diskos (series)

By Pete Hautman. Candlewick.

1. **The Obsidian Blade.** 2012.
2. **The Cydonian Pyramid.** 2013.

SCIENCE FICTION "The camel, the walled city, the way people were dressed all added up to his being somewhere in Africa or the Middle East. He wished he'd paid closer attention in his geography and history classes because, he thought with a sour smile, you never know when you might be magically transported halfway around the world and hundreds of years into the past."

Lamentation

By Ken Scholes. Tor, 2009.

FANTASY AND MAGICAL REALISM In a postapocalyptic world, centuries after the folly of man has pushed civilization to the brink, the world has been reordered and brought together again, until an ancient evil is recalled to destroy the center of this emerging civilization. Now all powers strive, in ways both forthright and subtle, to fill the void and dominate what is left over. At the center of the storm is a warrior of great destiny; a boy caught in the whirlwind; a woman who is being played like a game piece on a board; and a long-dead leader who has returned to this turbu-lent world in hopes of saving it. Passion, power, ambition, and enlightenment mix in a fast-paced tale of a world reborn.

Last Ride
By Laura Langston. Orca, 2011.

ACTION, ADVENTURE, AND MYSTERY; HI/LO; SPORTS Five thousand pounds of roaring, customized, racing machine: that's all Tom Shields has between him and the ghost of his dead friend, tens of thousands of dollars of debt, and the despair of the only girl he cares about. It isn't enough. *Last Ride* is raw, gutsy, and full of street-level reality.

The Less-Dead
By April Lurie. Delacorte, 2010.

ACTION, ADVENTURE, AND MYSTERY Noah's friend Will is one of the "less-dead," an outcast with no family, no home, a gay teen on the outside. No one will really care for a nobody in a pauper's grave once the headlines about his murder have passed. But Noah won't have it. He'll put it all on the line—his freedom, his family, even his life—to acknowledge the bright light that was his friend, and maybe stop the next murder.

The Leviathan Trilogy (series)
By Scott Westerfeld. Illustrated by Keith Thompson. Simon Pulse.

   1. *Leviathan.* 2009.
   2. *Behemoth.* 2010.
   3. *Goliath.* 2011.

MILITARY; SCIENCE FICTION The first real mainstream teen book with a steampunk sensibility, Westerfeld creates an alternate history world where World War I is fought between the half of the world that embraced Darwinism and the manipulation of life against the half that chose the path of steam and steel engineering.

Mangaman
By Barry Lyga. Illustrated by Colleen Doran. Houghton Mifflin, 2011.

COMICS, MANGA, AND GRAPHIC LITERATURE A sci-fi/manga retelling of *Romeo and Juliet*? With a nod to *Flat Stanley*? If you are a manga fan, try to imagine a manga character rocketed into our world from the two dimensional pages of a comic book world. Every thought bubble actually appears beside his head. Motion lines appear when he runs, then fall to the ground. And that thing they do with their eyes! Clever, fun, and beautifully drawn.

Marathon

By Boaz Yakin and Joe Infurnari. First Second, 2012.

COMICS, MANGA, AND GRAPHIC LITERATURE; HISTORICAL FICTION; MILITARY
One hundred ninety-two Athenians died on the plains of Marathon that day, and 6,500 Persians. Still, Athens would have fallen if not for the heroism and sacrifice of a few brave soldiers and the original Marathon champion. Here is their epic story, told brilliantly in comics.

Michael Vey (series)

By Richard Paul Evans. Simon Pulse.

1. *Michael Vey: The Prisoner of Cell 25.* 2011.
2. *Michael Vey: Rise of the Elgen.* 2012.

SCIENCE FICTION Oh, come on! Who wouldn't read a book about kids with electric superpowers?

Mickey Bolitar Novels (series)

By Harlan Coben. G. P. Putnam's Sons.

1. *Shelter.* 2011.
2. *Seconds Away.* 2012.

ACTION, ADVENTURE, AND MYSTERY Mickey Bolitar has lived all over the world and never gone to school. It would be nice to settle into being a normal teen for just a little while. Not going to happen . . . A mysterious old lady shouts strange and disturbing words from a haunted house, a man in a big black car seems to be following him, his father dies, and his girlfriend disappears. Oh, and I think I got whiplash on that last plot twist.

Monument 14

By Emmy Laybourne. Feiwel and Friends, 2012.

SCIENCE FICTION A teen-angst-fueled, apocalyptic, science fiction *Lord of the Flies.* Hold on, this is a wild ride.

Morpheus Road (series)

By D. J. MacHale. Aladdin.

1. *The Light.* 2010.
2. *The Black.* 2011.
3. *The Blood.* 2012.

GOTHIC HORROR, SUPERNATURAL, AND SUSPENSE Marsh is going crazy, or at least he hopes so. Crazy would be so much better than what he thinks is really going on. A character he created jumps off the page to wave a pick shovel at him; boats explode; walls of blood threaten to drown him. And if it is all in his head, then people he knows—and some he loves—may not be dead. This is a Stephen King–style thriller series from the author of the Pendragon series, and will have you covering your eyes, then peeking through to read the next hair-raising chapter.

Off Limits
By Robert Rayner. Lorimer, 2012.

ACTION, ADVENTURE, AND MYSTERY; HI/LO If it's forbidden, it's in here, so be forewarned. Deal with it; teens have to every day.

The Paladin Prophecy
By Mark Frost. Random House, 2012.

FANTASY AND MAGICAL REALISM; GOTHIC HORROR, SUPERNATURAL, AND SUSPENSE; SCIENCE FICTION A wild genre mash-up with enough Tolkien references for any fantasy fan, enough gadgetry for *Men in Black* sci-fi nuts, and enough creepy darkness for those gothic horror/Darren Shan aficionados. This is the first in a series.

Payback Time
By Carl Deuker. Houghton Mifflin, 2010.

SPORTS Something is definitely wrong with the Lincoln Mustang's new football player. He is great—when he wants to be. He wins games—when the coach plays him. He ducks the spotlight and won't let his picture be taken. With all the hype, and cheating, that surrounds big-time high school sports, a school newspaper reporter gets caught up in the mystery man's game, and so much more. Carl Deuker is the master of capturing the drama of sports, both on and off the field.

Pick-Up Game: A Full Day of Full Court
Edited by Marc Aronson and Charles R. Smith Jr. Candlewick, 2011.

SPORTS One day, one court, ten testaments to the drama inside the game and out. This is the home of pickup basketball, downtown Manhattan, where the immortals played when black players weren't allowed in big-time college basketball and the NBA. And still they come, troubled, homeless, too young, too old . . . nothing matters but your game when you step into The Cage.

Ready Player One
By Ernest Cline. Crown, 2011.

SCIENCE FICTION A futuristic video game world based on 1980s pop culture? One for parents and teens to read together (so the teens have someone to ask, "Dad, what is a Duran Duran?"). Pair it up with *Erebus* by Ursula Poznanski to compare two generations of video game madness.

The Relic Master (series)
By Catherine Fisher. Dial, 2011.

1. *The Dark City*
2. *The Lost Heiress*
3. *The Hidden Coronet*
4. *The Margrave*

FANTASY AND MAGICAL REALISM A sci-fi/fantasy mash-up of a world in fear of ancient and misunderstood relics of incredible technological power from a powerful lost civilization. A mystical order seeks to preserve and understand them, while a repressive power structure seeks to bury these relics of another age. Is it more dangerous to suppress this power, or to use it?

Replication: The Jason Experiment
By Jill Williamson. Zondervan, 2011.

CHRISTIAN FICTION; SCIENCE FICTION Jeremiah 1:5—"Before I formed you in the womb, I knew you." But what if it wasn't God that formed you? Cloning is more than an ethical and theoretical question in this science fiction thriller of a young man created to serve a purpose, but who looks for a greater one in a world that he can't understand—and that won't understand him.

The Return Man
By V. M. Zito. Orbit, 2012.

GOTHIC HORROR, SUPERNATURAL, AND SUSPENSE An adult book that will appeal to those teenage boys who love pure nonstop zombie apocalypse action. Forget complicated plots and in-depth characters; just bring on the ravenous undead.

Ripper
By Stefan Petrucha. Philomel, 2012.

ACTION, ADVENTURE, AND MYSTERY A teenage aspiring detective is hunting his father. A New York police commissioner is hunting a serial killer. A legendary

Pinkerton detective is hunting the most notorious killer who ever lived. When these investigations collide, the fallout is murder.

Robopocalypse
By Daniel H. Wilson. Doubleday, 2011.

SCIENCE FICTION What if your smart phone was smarter than you . . . and wanted you dead?

Rot and Ruin (series)
By Jonathan Maberry. Simon and Schuster.

    1. ***Rot and Ruin.*** 2010.
    2. ***Dust and Decay.*** 2011.
    3. ***Flesh and Bone.*** 2012.

GOTHIC HORROR, SUPERNATURAL, AND SUSPENSE In the midst of a zombie apocalypse, what if the most frightening thing were us? Just who are the monsters here anyway? It is good versus evil, but the zombies are neither. The good and evil are there within the humans; the zombies just bring out their true nature.

Scab
By Robert Rayner. Lorimer, 2010.

ACTION, ADVENTURE, AND MYSTERY; HI/LO Just think how bad your life would have to be as a high school senior if you preferred your camera to people. Then think how amazing you would be as a photographer. But what are the costs of holding on to a camera instead of reaching out to living, breathing people, especially those who need you?

The Second Base Club
By Greg Trine. Henry Holt, 2010.

HUMOR A lighter, more whimsical look at the high school jungle through a boy's eye.

Shadow on the Mountain
By Margi Preus. Amulet, 2012.

HISTORICAL FICTION; MILITARY Real people fought the Nazis in a thousand small ways, and the people of Norway were among those who fought the longest. The Nazis were sure that the blond-haired, blue-eyed people of Norway would welcome them with open arms, and there they would hold out until the end in "Fortress Norway." They were wrong. *Shadow on the Mountain,* based on actual stories of the Resistance, shows the heroic courage of those who not only fought the Nazis, but refused to lose what made them better than their enemies to begin with.

Sidekicks

By Jack D. Ferraiolo. Amulet, 2011.

HUMOR; SCIENCE FICTION What do you call the dorkiest, silliest-looking, must socially inept sidekick to ever face off with his partner against evil? A hero . . .

Soldier Bear

By Bibi Dumon Tak. Translated by Laura Watkinson. Illustrated by Philip Hopman. Eerdmans, 2011.

HISTORICAL FICTION; MILITARY Who would have imagined that the most human thing in an inhuman war would end up being a bear? Based on the true story of a bear that was adopted by a Polish army unit in World War II.

Swim the Fly (series)

By Don Calame. Candlewick.

1. *Swim the Fly.* 2009.
2. *Beat the Band.* 2010.
3. *Call the Shots.* 2012.

HUMOR When I recommend a teen angst novel, or a series of them, with all the old standbys—dorky guy who doesn't have a chance with the way-too-hot girl with the big gorilla-ish boyfriend who is sure to beat the snot out of the dorky guy—well, you know it is special. *Swim the Fly, Beat the Band,* and *Call the Shots* are unapologetically teen angst novels that are just so over-the-top funny they have to be experienced. And it is guy humor too: bathroom and bodily function jokes, stupid pranks, and insanely complex schemes that go horribly wrong. So laugh it up with three loser friends who have vowed that this is the summer they will see . . . well, you'll figure it out.

Thou Shalt Not Road Trip

By Antony John. Dial, 2012.

CHRISTIAN FICTION; HUMOR How can you have a Christian book with alcohol, tattoos, and teen hormones? Well, that's sort of the point. Luke really is a faithful Christian 16-year-old, and he has written a wildly popular inspirational, idealized book for kids. But how do ideals survive in the real world, away from the comfort and guidance of parents, pastor, and church? How does a Christian teen survive in an un-Christian world?

Touched

By Cyn Balog. Delacorte, 2012.

FANTASY AND MAGICAL REALISM Nick Cross remembers getting married, having kids and grandkids, and growing old. He also remembers becoming a crack addict in a loveless marriage to a Vegas stripper and being murdered in a drug deal in his early 20s. Nick remembers many lives, none of which have happened . . . yet. Nick is just 18 years old.

True Legend

By Mike Lupica. Philomel, 2012.

SPORTS It's good to be The Man. People write your papers, buy you things, drive you everywhere you want to go, and take care of those little "problems" that sometimes come up. Drew "True" Robinson is enjoying the perks of being the next great basketball prospect when he meets a ghost on a dark outdoor court one night: mad skills, grubby clothes, a haunted look. But is it the ghost of a failed prospect past? Or the ghost of Drew's future?

20th Century Boys

By Naoki Urasawa. VIZ Media, 2009–. (Manga)

COMICS, MANGA, AND GRAPHIC LITERATURE A group of boys play at good guys and bad guys in their own secluded club. Child stuff, right? But as adults, the evil they invented becomes all too real, and only one of the original friends can be behind it. Who grew up to be an evil genius? And what does it mean for the only people who know the origin of that evil?

Unholy Night

By Seth Grahame-Smith. Grand Central Publishing, 2012.

CHRISTIAN FICTION; GOTHIC HORROR, SUPERNATURAL, AND SUSPENSE The author of *Pride and Prejudice and Zombies* and *Abraham Lincoln: Vampire Hunter* brings a gothic sensibility to, of all things, the Nativity story. Forbidden magic, torture, swarms of homicidal insects—what dark secrets may lurk behind the ultimate story of peace and hope? The presence of the Holy Family forms a stark contrast to the dark forces that array against it, making for a clearer battle of good and evil than usual in Christian or gothic books.

The Unwind Trilogy (series)
By Neal Shusterman. Simon and Schuster.

1. *Unwind.* 2009.
2. *UnWholly.* 2012.
3. *UnSouled.* 2013.

SCIENCE FICTION In a world not too far in the future, America has finally solved the abortion debate once and for all. We won't abort babies. We will abort teenagers.

Vietnam (series)
By Chris Lynch. Scholastic.

1. *I Pledge Allegiance.* 2011.
2. *Sharpshooter.* 2012.
3. *Free-Fire Zone.* 2012.
4. *Casualties of War.* 2013.

HISTORICAL FICTION; MILITARY "There are no Zippo boats there yet, boys, and the nearest jets carrying napalm got blown away on the ground. VC are entrenched in Mangrove swamps and jungle and tunnels so deep, they must've been living there for years, waiting. Everybody is waiting on us, and we are letting men die every extra second. I can promise you this, men. You have never been more needed in your entire sorry lives than you are needed right this minute."

The Wager
By Donna Jo Napoli. Henry Holt, 2010.

GOTHIC HORROR, SUPERNATURAL, AND SUSPENSE This retelling of the ancient story of Faust adds a new twist to the idea of betting against the devil. How long could you go without taking a bath?

Zombies vs. Unicorns
Edited by Holly Black and Justine Larbalestier. Margaret K. McElderry, 2010.

FANTASY AND MAGICAL REALISM; GOTHIC HORROR, SUPERNATURAL, AND SUSPENSE Don't be fooled into thinking these stories fall into predictable lines, with girly unicorns and blood-thirsty zombies. Garth Nix and Kathleen Duey bat for Team Unicorn. Libra Bray is on Team Zombie. Unicorns are sometimes vicious killers, and zombies fall in love. For the three people who ever before dreamed of a zombie/unicorn book, you never dreamed it would be like this. Three words: Rainbow . . . farting . . . unicorns!

Books by Genre and Subject

Action, Adventure, and Mystery

Elementary

The Case of the Vanishing Golden Frogs: A Scientific Mystery. By Sandra Markle. Millbrook Press, 2012.

Disaster Survivors (series). Bearport, 2010.

1. *Blitzed by a Blizzard!* By Joyce L. Markovics.
2. *Devastated by a Volcano!* By Stephen Person.
3. *Erased by a Tornado!* By Jessica Rudolph.
4. *Hammered by a Heat Wave!* By Laura DeLallo.
5. *Leveled by an Earthquake!* By Adam Reingold.
6. *Mangled by a Hurricane!* By Miriam Aronin.
7. *Slammed by a Tsunami!* By Miriam Aronin.
8. *Struck by Lightning!* By Stephen Person.

The Work of Heroes: First Responders in Action (series). Bearport.

1. *Doctors to the Rescue.* By Meish Goldish. 2012.
2. *Firefighters to the Rescue.* By Meish Goldish. 2012.
3. *Paramedics to the Rescue.* By Nancy White. 2012.
4. *Police Officers to the Rescue.* By Nancy White. 2012.
5. *Animal Control Officers to the Rescue.* By Meish Goldish. 2013.
6. *Wildlife Rehabilitators to the Rescue.* By Meish Goldish. 2013.

Middle School

Adventure Beneath the Sea: Living in an Underwater Science Station. By Kenneth Mallory. Photographs by Brian Skerry. Boyds Mills Press, 2010.

Island of Thieves. By Josh Lacey. Houghton Mifflin, 2012.

Jason Steed (series). By Mark A. Cooper. Sourcebooks Jabberwocky.

1. *Fledgling.* 2010.
2. *Revenge.* 2012.

No Place like Holmes (series). By Jason Lethcoe. Thomas Nelson, 2011.

1. *No Place like Holmes*
2. *The Future Door*

Storm Runners (series). By Roland Smith. Scholastic.

    1. *Storm Runners*. 2011.

    2. *The Surge*. 2011.

    3. *Eruption*. 2012.

Take Me to the River. By Will Hobbs. Harper, 2011.

The Ultimate Survival Guide. By Mike Flynn. Illustrated by Mike Phillips. Macmillan, 2010.

Wild Rescue (series). By J. Burchett and S. Vogler. Illustrated by Diane Le Feyer. Stone Arch, 2012.

    1. *Poacher Panic*

    2. *Earthquake Escape*

    3. *Rainforest Rescue*

    4. *Polar Meltdown*

    5. *Safari Survival*

    6. *Ocean S.O.S.*

    7. *Avalanche Alert*

    8. *Desert Danger*

High School

Angry Young Man. By Chris Lynch. Simon and Schuster, 2011.

Au Revoir, Crazy European Chick. By Joe Schreiber. Houghton Mifflin, 2011.

Blacksad. By Juan Diaz Canales and Juanjo Guarnido. Dark Horse, 2010.

Boy21. By Matthew Quick. Little, Brown, 2012.

Chew (series). By John Layman and Rob Guillory. Image Comics.

    1. *Taster's Choice*. 2009.

    2. *International Flavor*. 2010.

    3. *Just Desserts*. 2010.

    4. *Flambé*. 2011.

    5. *Major League Chew*. 2012.

    6. *Space Cakes*. 2013.

The Coldest City. By Antony Johnston. Illustrated by Sam Hart. Oni Press, 2012.

Guilty. By Norah McClintock. Orca, 2012.

Last Ride. By Laura Langston. Orca, 2011.

The Less-Dead. By April Lurie. Delacorte, 2010.

The Lost City of Z: A Tale of Deadly Obsession in the Amazon. By David Grann. Doubleday, 2009.

Mickey Bolitar Novels (series). By Harlan Coben. G. P. Putnam's Sons.

    1. *Shelter*. 2011.

    2. *Seconds Away*. 2012.

Off Limits. By Robert Rayner. Lorimer, 2012.

Perry's Killer Playlist. By Joe Schreiber. Houghton Mifflin, 2012.

Ripper. By Stefan Petrucha. Philomel, 2012.

Scab. By Robert Rayner. Lorimer, 2010.

Animals

Elementary

Afraid of the Water (series). Bearport, 2010.

1. *Blue-Ringed Octopus: Small but Deadly.* By Natalie Lunis.

2. *Box Jellyfish: Killer Tentacles.* By Natalie Lunis.

3. *Moray Eel: Dangerous Teeth.* By Meish Goldish.

4. *Portuguese Man-of-War: Floating Misery.* By Natalie Lunis.

5. *Shark: The Shredder.* By Meish Goldish.

6. *Stonefish: Needles of Pain.* By Meish Goldish.

Baby Mammoth Mummy: Frozen in Time! A Prehistoric Animal's Journey into the 21st Century. By Christopher Sloan with Bernard Buigues. Photographs by Francis Latreille. National Geographic, 2011.

Barnum's Bones: How Barnum Brown Discovered the Most Famous Dinosaur in the World. By Tracy Fern. Illustrated by Boris Kulikov. Farrar, Straus and Giroux, 2012.

Big Cats: In Search of Lions, Leopards, Cheetahs, and Tigers. By Steve Bloom. Thames and Hudson, 2012.

Biggest, Baddest Book of Beasts. By Anders Hanson and Elissa Mann. ABDO, 2013.

The Case of the Vanishing Golden Frogs: A Scientific Mystery. By Sandra Markle. Millbrook Press, 2012.

Dogs on Duty: Soldiers' Best Friends on the Battlefield and Beyond. By Dorothy Hinshaw Patent. Walker, 2012.

The Flying Beaver Brothers (series). By Maxwell Eaton III. Knopf.

1. *The Flying Beaver Brothers and the Evil Penguin Plan.* 2012.

2. *The Flying Beaver Brothers and the Fishy Business.* 2012.

3. *The Flying Beaver Brothers and the Mud-Slinging Moles.* 2013.

4. *The Flying Beaver Brothers: Birds vs. Bunnies.* 2013.

Just Joking: 300 Hilarious Jokes, Tricky Tongue Twisters, and Ridiculous Riddles. National Geographic, 2012.

Just Joking 2: 300 Hilarious Jokes about Everything, Including Tongue Twisters, Riddles, and More! National Geographic, 2012.

Mysteries of the Komodo Dragon: The Biggest, Deadliest Lizard Gives Up Its Secrets. By Marty Crump. Boyds Mills Press, 2010.

Saving the Baghdad Zoo: A True Story of Hope and Heroes. By Kelly Milner Halls and William Sumner. Greenwillow, 2010.

Stone Rabbit (series). By Erik Craddock. Random House.

1. *BC Mambo.* 2009.

2. *Pirate Palooza.* 2009.

3. *Deep-Space Disco.* 2009.

4. *Superhero Stampede.* 2010.

5. *Ninja Slice.* 2010.

6. *Night of the Living Dust Bunnies.* 2011.

7. *Dragon Boogie.* 2012.

8. *Robot Frenzy.* 2013.

Middle School

Awesome Snake Science! 40 Activities for Learning about Snakes. By Cindy Blobaum. Chicago Review Press, 2012.

Chomp. By Carl Hiaasen. Knopf, 2012.

50 Poisonous Questions: A Book with Bite. By Tanya Lloyd Kyi. Illustrated by Ross Kinnaird. Annick Press, 2011.

Here There Be Monsters: The Legendary Kraken and the Giant Squid. By H. P. Newquist. Houghton Mifflin, 2010.

Mush! Sled Dogs with Issues. By Glenn Eichler and Joe Infurnari. First Second, 2011.

Wild Rescue (series). By J. Burchett and S. Vogler. Illustrated by Diane Le Feyer. Stone Arch, 2012.

1. *Poacher Panic*

2. *Earthquake Escape*

3. *Rainforest Rescue*

4. *Polar Meltdown*

5. *Safari Survival*

6. *Ocean S.O.S.*

7. *Avalanche Alert*

8. *Desert Danger*

High School

Bulu: African Wonder Dog. By Dick Houston. Random House, 2010.

Soldier Bear. By Bibi Dumon Tak. Translated by Laura Watkinson. Illustrated by Philip Hopman. Eerdmans, 2011.

Soldier Dogs: The Untold Story of America's Canine Heroes. By Maria Goodavage. Dutton, 2012.

Biography, Autobiography, and Memoir

Elementary

Barnum's Bones: How Barnum Brown Discovered the Most Famous Dinosaur in the World. By Tracy Fern. Illustrated by Boris Kulikov. Farrar, Straus and Giroux, 2012.

Brothers at Bat: The True Story of an Amazing All-Brother Baseball Team. By Audrey Vernick. Illustrated by Steven Salerno. Clarion, 2012.

No Easy Way: The Story of Ted Williams and the Last .400 Season. By Fred Bowen. Illustrated by Charles S. Pyle. Dutton, 2010.

Spirit Seeker: John Coltrane's Musical Journey. By Gary Golio. Paintings by Rudy Gutierrez. Clarion, 2012.

The Work of Heroes: First Responders in Action (series). Bearport.

1. *Doctors to the Rescue*. By Meish Goldish. 2012.

2. *Firefighters to the Rescue*. By Meish Goldish. 2012.

3. *Paramedics to the Rescue*. By Nancy White. 2012.

4. *Police Officers to the Rescue*. By Nancy White. 2012.

5. *Animal Control Officers to the Rescue*. By Meish Goldish. 2013.

6. *Wildlife Rehabilitators to the Rescue*. By Meish Goldish. 2013.

X-Moves (series). By Michael Sandler. Bearport, 2010.

1. *Cool Snowboarders*

2. *Daring BMXers*

3. *Gnarly Skateboarders*

4. *Mighty MotoXers*

5. *Rally Car Dudes*

6. *Super Surfers*

Middle School

Albert Einstein and Relativity for Kids: His Life and Ideas with 21 Activities and Thought Experiments. By Jerome Pohlen. Chicago Review Press, 2012.

Candy Bomber: The Story of the Berlin Airlift's "Chocolate Pilot." By Michael O. Tunnell. Charlesbridge, 2010.

Frederick Douglass for Kids: His Life and Times with 21 Activities. By Nancy I. Sanders. Chicago Review Press, 2012.

Hammerin' Hank Greenberg: Baseball Pioneer. By Shelley Sommer. Calkins Creek, 2011.

How They Croaked: The Awful Ends of the Awfully Famous. By Georgia Bragg. Illustrated by Kevin O'Malley. Walker, 2011.

Lincoln's Flying Spies: Thaddeus Lowe and the Civil War Balloon Corps. By Gail Jarrow. Calkins Creek, 2010.

High School

Bulu: African Wonder Dog. By Dick Houston. Random House, 2010.

Fist Stick Knife Gun: A Personal History of Violence. By Geoffrey Canada. Adapted by Jamar Nicholas. Beacon Press, 2010.

My Friend Dahmer. By Derf Backderf. Abrams ComicArts, 2012.

Signing Their Rights Away: The Fame and Misfortune of the Men Who Signed the United States Constitution. By Denise Kiernan and Joseph D'Agnese. Quirk Books, 2011.

The Warrior's Heart: Becoming a Man of Compassion and Courage. By Eric Greitens. Houghton Mifflin, 2012.

Christian Fiction

Elementary

Escape by Night: A Civil War Adventure (Historical Fiction). By Laurie Myers. Illustrated by Amy June Bates. Henry Holt, 2011.

The Imagination Station (series) (Fantasy). Tyndale House.

1. *Voyage with the Vikings.* By Marianne Hering and Paul McCusker. Illustrated by David Hohn. 2010.

2. *Attack at the Arena.* By Marianne Hering and Paul McCusker. Illustrated by David Hohn. 2010.

3. *Peril in the Palace.* By Marianne Hering and Paul McCusker. Illustrated by David Hohn. 2011.

4. *Revenge of the Red Knight.* By Marianne Hering and Paul McCusker. Illustrated by David Hohn. 2011.

5. *Showdown with the Shepherd.* By Marianne Hering and Brock Eastman. Illustrated by David Hohn. 2011.

6. *Problems in Plymouth.* By Marianne Hering and Marshal Younger. Illustrated by David Hohn. 2011.

7. *Secret of the Prince's Tomb.* By Marianne Hering and Marshal Younger. Illustrated by David Hohn. 2012.

8. *Battle for Cannibal Island.* By Marianne Hering and Wayne Thomas Batson. Illustrated by David Hohn. 2012.

9. *Escape to the Hiding Place.* By Marianne Hering and Marshal Younger. Illustrated by David Hohn. 2012.

10. *Challenge on the Hill of Fire.* By Marianne Hering and Nancy I. Sanders. Illustrated by David Hohn. 2012.

Middle School

The Berinfell Prophecies (series) (Fantasy). By Wayne Thomas Batson and Christopher Hopper. Thomas Nelson.

1. *Curse of the Spider King.* 2009.

2. *Venom and Song.* 2010.

3. *The Tide of Unmaking.* 2012.

No Place like Holmes (series) (Mystery). By Jason Lethcoe. Thomas Nelson, 2011.

    1. *No Place like Holmes*

    2. *The Future Door*

Son of Angels, Jonah Stone (series) (Gothic/Horror). By Jerel Law. Thomas Nelson.

    1. *Spirit Fighter*. 2011.

    2. *Fire Prophet*. 2012.

    3. *Shadow Chaser*. 2013.

High School

Crater: A Helium-3 Novel. By Homer Hickam. Thomas Nelson, 2012. (Science Fiction)

Crazy Dangerous. By Andrew Klavan. Thomas Nelson, 2012. (Gothic/Horror)

Days of Little Texas. By R. A. Nelson. Knopf, 2009. (Gothic/Horror)

Failstate. By John W. Otte. Marcher Lord, 2012. (Science Fiction)

Replication: The Jason Experiment. By Jill Williamson. Zondervan, 2011. (Science Fiction)

Thou Shalt Not Road Trip. By Antony John. Dial, 2012. (Humor)

Unholy Night. By Seth Grahame-Smith. Grand Central Publishing, 2012. (Gothic/Horror)

Comics, Manga, and Graphic Literature

Elementary

The Adventures of Ook and Gluk: Kung-Fu Cavemen from the Future. By Dav Pilkey. Blue Sky Press, 2010.

The Cartoon Chronicles of America (series). By Stan Mack and Susan Champlin. Bloomsbury.

    1. *Road to Revolution.* 2009.

    2. *Fight for Freedom.* 2012.

Darth Vader and Son. By Jeffrey Brown. Chronicle Books, 2012.

Dragonbreath (series). By Ursula Vernon. Dial.

    1. *Dragonbreath.* 2009.

    2. *Attack of the Ninja Frogs.* 2010.

    3. *Curse of the Were-Wiener.* 2010.

    4. *Lair of the Bat Monster.* 2011.

    5. *No Such Thing as Ghosts.* 2011.

    6. *Revenge of the Horned Bunnies.* 2012.

    7. *When Fairies Go Bad.* 2012.

    8. *Nightmare of the Iguana.* 2013.

    9. *The Case of the Toxic Mutant.* 2013.

The Flying Beaver Brothers (series). By Maxwell Eaton III. Knopf.

    1. *The Flying Beaver Brothers and the Evil Penguin Plan.* 2012.

    2. *The Flying Beaver Brothers and the Fishy Business.* 2012.

    3. *The Flying Beaver Brothers and the Mud-Slinging Moles.* 2013.

    4. *The Flying Beaver Brothers: Birds vs. Bunnies.* 2013.

Lunch Lady (series). By Jarrett J. Krosoczka. Knopf.

    1. *Lunch Lady and the Cyborg Substitute.* 2009.

    2. *Lunch Lady and the League of Librarians.* 2009.

    3. *Lunch Lady and the Author Visit Vendetta.* 2009.

    4. *Lunch Lady and the Summer Camp Shakedown.* 2010.

    5. *Lunch Lady and the Bake Sale Bandit.* 2010.

    6. *Lunch Lady and the Field Trip Fiasco.* 2011.

    7. *Lunch Lady and the Mutant Mathletes.* 2012.

    8. *Lunch Lady and the Picture Day Peril.* 2012.

    9. *Lunch Lady and the Video Game Villain.* 2013.

Stone Rabbit (series). By Erik Craddock. Random House.

1. *BC Mambo*. 2009.
2. *Pirate Palooza*. 2009.
3. *Deep-Space Disco*. 2009.
4. *Superhero Stampede*. 2010.
5. *Ninja Slice*. 2010.
6. *Night of the Living Dust Bunnies*. 2011.
7. *Dragon Boogie*. 2012.
8. *Robot Frenzy*. 2013.

Middle School

Bad Island. By Doug TenNapel. Graphix, 2011.

Big Nate (series). By Lincoln Peirce. Harper.

1. *Big Nate: In a Class by Himself*. 2010.
2. *Big Nate Strikes Again*. 2010.
3. *Big Nate on a Roll*. 2011.
4. *Big Nate Goes for Broke*. 2012.
5. *Big Nate: What Could Possibly Go Wrong?* 2012.
6. *Big Nate: Here Goes Nothing*. 2012.
7. *Big Nate Flips Out*. 2013.

Cardboard. By Doug TenNapel. Graphix, 2012.

Ghostopolis. By Doug TenNapel. Graphix, 2010.

Mush! Sled Dogs with Issues. By Glenn Eichler and Joe Infurnari. First Second, 2011.

High School

American Vampire. By Scott Snyder and Rafael Albuquerque. Vertigo, 2010–. (Graphic series)

Blacksad. By Juan Diaz Canales and Juanjo Guarnido. Dark Horse, 2010.

Brody's Ghost. By Mark Crilley. Dark Horse, 2010–. (Manga)

Cage of Eden. By Yoshinobu Yamada. Translated by Mari Morimoto. Kodansha Comics, 2011–. (Manga)

Chew (series). By John Layman and Rob Guillory. Image Comics.

    1. *Taster's Choice*. 2009.

    2. *International Flavor*. 2010.

    3. *Just Desserts*. 2010.

    4. *Flambé*. 2011.

    5. *Major League Chew*. 2012.

    6. *Space Cakes*. 2013.

The Coldest City. By Antony Johnston. Illustrated by Sam Hart. Oni Press, 2012.

Dawn Land. By Joseph Bruchac. Adapted and illustrated by Will Davis. First Second, 2010.

Fist Stick Knife Gun: A Personal History of Violence. By Geoffrey Canada. Adapted by Jamar Nicholas. Beacon Press, 2010.

The Griff. By Christopher Moore and Ian Corson with Jennyson Rosero. William Morrow, 2011.

Habibi. By Craig Thompson. Pantheon, 2011.

Ikigami: The Ultimate Limit. By Motoro Mase. VIZ Media, 2009–. (Manga)

Mangaman. By Barry Lyga. Illustrated by Colleen Doran. Houghton Mifflin, 2011.

Marathon. By Boaz Yakin and Joe Infurnari. First Second, 2012.

My Friend Dahmer. By Derf Backderf. Abrams ComicArts, 2012.

Still I Rise: A Graphic History of African Americans. By Roland Laird with Taneshia Nash Laird. Illustrated by Elihu "Adofo" Bey. Sterling, 2009.

Taxes, the Tea Party, and Those Revolting Rebels: A History in Comics of the American Revolution. By Stan Mack. Nantier, Beall, Minoustchine, 2012.

20th Century Boys. By Naoki Urasawa. VIZ Media, 2009–. (Manga)

Fantasy and Magical Realism

Elementary

The Imagination Station (series). Tyndale House.

1. *Voyage with the Vikings.* By Marianne Hering and Paul McCusker. Illustrated by David Hohn. 2010.

2. *Attack at the Arena.* By Marianne Hering and Paul McCusker. Illustrated by David Hohn. 2010.

3. *Peril in the Palace.* By Marianne Hering and Paul McCusker. Illustrated by David Hohn. 2011.

4. *Revenge of the Red Knight.* By Marianne Hering and Paul McCusker. Illustrated by David Hohn. 2011.

5. *Showdown with the Shepherd.* By Marianne Hering and Brock Eastman. Illustrated by David Hohn. 2011.

6. *Problems in Plymouth.* By Marianne Hering and Marshal Younger. Illustrated by David Hohn. 2011.

7. *Secret of the Prince's Tomb.* By Marianne Hering and Marshal Younger. Illustrated by David Hohn. 2012.

8. *Battle for Cannibal Island.* By Marianne Hering and Wayne Thomas Batson. Illustrated by David Hohn. 2012.

9. *Escape to the Hiding Place.* By Marianne Hering and Marshal Younger. Illustrated by David Hohn. 2012.

10. *Challenge on the Hill of Fire.* By Marianne Hering and Nancy I. Sanders. Illustrated by David Hohn. 2012.

Leprechauns and Irish Folklore: A Nonfiction Companion to "Leprechaun in Late Winter." By Mary Pope Osborne and Natalie Pope Boyce. Illustrated by Sal Murdocca. Random House, 2010.

The Sapphire Knight. By Michael Sullivan. Illustrated by Douglas Sirois. PublishingWorks, 2009.

Underworlds (series). By Tony Abbott. Illustrated by Antonio Javier Caparo. Scholastic.

1. *The Battle Begins.* 2011.

2. *When Monsters Escape.* 2012.

3. *Revenge of the Scorpion King.* 2012.

4. *The Ice Dragon.* 2012.

Middle School

The Berinfell Prophecies (series). By Wayne Thomas Batson and Christopher Hopper. Thomas Nelson.

> 1. *Curse of the Spider King.* 2009.
>
> 2. *Venom and Song.* 2010.
>
> 3. *The Tide of Unmaking.* 2012.

The Brotherband Chronicles (series). By John Flanagan. Philomel.

> 1. *The Outcasts.* 2011.
>
> 2. *The Invaders.* 2012.
>
> 3. *The Hunters.* 2012.

Ghostopolis. By Doug TenNapel. Graphix, 2010.

The Heroes of Olympus (series). By Rick Riordan. Disney/Hyperion.

> 1. *The Lost Hero.* 2010.
>
> 2. *The Son of Neptune.* 2011.
>
> 3. *The Mark of Athena.* 2012.
>
> 4. *The Demigod Diaries.* 2012.

The Kane Chronicles (series). By Rick Riordan. Disney/Hyperion.

> 1. *The Red Pyramid.* 2010.
>
> 2. *The Throne of Fire.* 2011.
>
> 3. *The Serpent's Shadow.* 2012.
>
> 4. *The Kane Chronicles Survival Guide.* Written by Mary-Jane Knight. Illustrated by Antonio Caparo, Philip Chidlow, and Artful Doodlers. 2012.

The Last Musketeer. By Stuart Gibbs. Harper, 2011.

The Ring of Solomon: A Bartimaeus Novel. By Jonathan Stroud. Disney/Hyperion, 2010.

High School

The Ascendance Trilogy (series). By Jennifer A. Nielsen. Scholastic.

> 1. *The False Prince.* 2012.
>
> 2. *The Runaway King.* 2013.

Bruiser. By Neal Shusterman. HarperTeen, 2010.

Flip. By Martyn Bedford. Wendy Lamb, 2011.

Lamentation. By Ken Scholes. Tor, 2009.

The Paladin Prophecy. By Mark Frost. Random House, 2012.

The Relic Master (series). By Catherine Fisher. Dial, 2011.

    1. *The Dark City*

    2. *The Lost Heiress*

    3. *The Hidden Coronet*

    4. *The Margrave*

Touched. By Cyn Balog. Delacorte, 2012.

Zombies vs. Unicorns. Edited by Holly Black and Justine Larbalestier. Margaret K. McElderry, 2010.

Gothic, Horror, Supernatural, and Suspense

Elementary

Ghost Buddy (series). By Henry Winkler and Lin Oliver. Scholastic.

    1. *Zero to Hero*. 2012.

    2. *Mind If I Read Your Mind?* 2012.

    3. *How to Scare the Pants Off Your Pets*. 2013.

Ghosts: A Nonfiction Companion to "A Good Night for Ghosts." By Mary Pope Osborne and Natalie Pope Boyce. Illustrated by Sal Murdocca. Random House, 2009.

Grizzly Tales: Cautionary Tales for Lovers of Squeam (series). By Jamie Rix. Orion.

    1. *Nasty Little Beasts*. 2010.

    2. *Gruesome Grown Ups*. 2010.

    3. *The "ME!" Monsters*. 2010.

    4. *Freaks of Nature*. 2010.

    5. *Terror Time Toys*. 2010.

    6. *Blubbers and Sicksters*. 2010.

    7. *The Gnaughty Gnomes of "No!"* 2010.

    8. *Superzeroes*. 2010.

The Haunting of Derek Stone (series). By Tony Abbott. Scholastic, 2009.

    1. *City of the Dead*

    2. *Bayou Dogs*

    3. *The Red House*

    4. *The Ghost Road*

Jack and Jill Went Up to Kill: A Book of Zombie Nursery Rhymes. By Michael P. Spradlin. Illustrated by Jeff Weigel. Harper, 2011.

Middle School

Cardboard. By Doug TenNapel. Graphix, 2012.

The Ghost of Graylock. By Dan Poblocki. Scholastic, 2012.

HorrorScapes (series). Bearport, 2011.

    1. *Dracula's Dark World*. By Michael Burgan.

    2. *Ghostly Alcatraz Island*. By Stephen Person.

    3. *Tut's Deadly Tomb*. By Natalie Lunis.

    4. *Voodoo in New Orleans*. By Stephen Person.

    5. *Witchcraft in Salem*. By Steven L. Stern.

A Monster Calls. By Patrick Ness. Candlewick, 2011.

On the Day I Died: Stories from the Grave. By Candice Fleming. Schwartz and Wade, 2012.

Son of Angels, Jonah Stone (series). By Jerel Law. Thomas Nelson.

    1. *Spirit Fighter*. 2011.

    2. *Fire Prophet*. 2012.

    3. *Shadow Chaser*. 2013.

Tales from Lovecraft Middle School (series). By Charles Gilman. Illustrated by Eugene Smith. Quirk Books.

    1. *Professor Gargoyle*. 2012.

    2. *The Slither Sisters*. 2013.

    3. *Teacher's Pest*. 2013.

The Thin Executioner. By Darren Shan. Little, Brown, 2010.

High School

American Vampire. By Scott Snyder and Rafael Albuquerque. Vertigo, 2010–. (Graphic series)

The Apprenticeship of Victor Frankenstein (series). By Kenneth Oppel. Simon and Schuster.

    1. *This Dark Endeavor*. 2011.

    2. *Such Wicked Intent*. 2012.

Brody's Ghost. By Mark Crilley. Dark Horse, 2010–. (Manga)

Crazy Dangerous. By Andrew Klavan. Thomas Nelson, 2012.

Croak (series). By Gina Damico. Graphia, 2012.

    1. *Croak*

    2. *Scorch*

Days of Little Texas. By R. A. Nelson. Knopf, 2009.

The Hunt (series). By Andrew Fukuda. St. Martin's Griffin.

    1. *The Hunt.* 2012.

    2. *The Prey.* 2013.

Morpheus Road (series). By D. J. MacHale. Aladdin.

    1. *The Light.* 2010.

    2. *The Black.* 2011.

    3. *The Blood.* 2012.

The Paladin Prophecy. By Mark Frost. Random House, 2012.

The Return Man. By V. M. Zito. Orbit, 2012.

Rot and Ruin (series). By Jonathan Maberry. Simon and Schuster.

    1. *Rot and Ruin.* 2010.

    2. *Dust and Decay.* 2011.

    3. *Flesh and Bone.* 2012.

Unholy Night. By Seth Grahame-Smith. Grand Central Publishing, 2012.

The Wager. By Donna Jo Napoli. Henry Holt, 2010.

Zombies vs. Unicorns. Edited by Holly Black and Justine Larbalestier. Margaret K. McElderry, 2010.

Hi/Lo (High Interest, Low Reading Level)

Elementary

Afraid of the Water (series). Bearport, 2010.

    1. *Blue-Ringed Octopus: Small but Deadly*. By Natalie Lunis.

    2. *Box Jellyfish: Killer Tentacles*. By Natalie Lunis.

    3. *Moray Eel: Dangerous Teeth*. By Meish Goldish.

    4. *Portuguese Man-of-War: Floating Misery*. By Natalie Lunis.

    5. *Shark: The Shredder*. By Meish Goldish.

    6. *Stonefish: Needles of Pain*. By Meish Goldish.

Disaster Survivors (series). Bearport, 2010.

    1. *Blitzed by a Blizzard!* By Joyce L. Markovics.

    2. *Devastated by a Volcano!* By Stephen Person.

    3. *Erased by a Tornado!* By Jessica Rudolph.

    4. *Hammered by a Heat Wave!* By Laura DeLallo.

    5. *Leveled by an Earthquake!* By Adam Reingold.

    6. *Mangled by a Hurricane!* By Miriam Aronin.

    7. *Slammed by a Tsunami!* By Miriam Aronin.

    8. *Struck by Lightning!* By Stephen Person.

Fast Rides (series). By Michael Sandler. Bearport, 2011.

    1. *Dynamic Drag Racers*

    2. *Electrifying Eco-Race Cars*

    3. *Hot Hot Rods*

    4. *Jet-Powered Speed*

The Work of Heroes: First Responders in Action (series). Bearport.

    1. *Doctors to the Rescue*. By Meish Goldish. 2012.

    2. *Firefighters to the Rescue*. By Meish Goldish. 2012.

    3. *Paramedics to the Rescue*. By Nancy White. 2012.

    4. *Police Officers to the Rescue*. By Nancy White. 2012.

    5. *Animal Control Officers to the Rescue*. By Meish Goldish. 2013.

    6. *Wildlife Rehabilitators to the Rescue*. By Meish Goldish. 2013.

X-Moves (series). By Michael Sandler. Bearport, 2010.

1. *Cool Snowboarders*

2. *Daring BMXers*

3. *Gnarly Skateboarders*

4. *Mighty MotoXers*

5. *Rally Car Dudes*

6. *Super Surfers*

Middle School

HorrorScapes (series). Bearport, 2011.

1. *Dracula's Dark World*. By Michael Burgan.

2. *Ghostly Alcatraz Island*. By Stephen Person.

3. *Tut's Deadly Tomb*. By Natalie Lunis.

4. *Voodoo in New Orleans*. By Stephen Person.

5. *Witchcraft in Salem*. By Steven L. Stern.

Nightmare Plagues (series). Bearport, 2011.

1. *Bubonic Plague: The Black Death!* By Stephen Person.

2. *The Flu of 1918: Millions Dead Worldwide!* By Jessica Rudolph.

3. *Malaria: Super Killer!* By Stephen Person.

4. *Smallpox: Is It Over?* By Adam Reingold.

5. *Tuberculosis: The White Plague!* By Miriam Aronin.

6. *Typhoid Fever: Dirty Food, Dirty Water!* By William Caper.

Playing for Keeps. By Steven Sandor. Lorimer, 2012.

True Tales of the Wild West (series). By Jeff Savage. Enslow, 2012.

1. American Cowboys

2. Daring Pony Express Riders

3. Fearless Scouts

4. Pioneering Women

5. Quick-Draw Gunfighters

6. *Rugged Gold Miners*

Wild Rescue (series). By J. Burchett and S. Vogler. Illustrated by Diane Le Feyer. Stone Arch, 2012.

1. *Poacher Panic*

2. *Earthquake Escape*

3. *Rainforest Rescue*

4. *Polar Meltdown*

5. *Safari Survival*

6. *Ocean S.O.S.*

7. *Avalanche Alert*

8. *Desert Danger*

High School

Guilty. By Norah McClintock. Orca, 2012.

Last Ride. By Laura Langston. Orca, 2011.

Off Limits. By Robert Rayner. Lorimer, 2012.

Scab. By Robert Rayner. Lorimer, 2010.

Historical Fiction

Elementary

The Cartoon Chronicles of America (series). By Stan Mack and Susan Champlin. Bloomsbury.

    1. *Road to Revolution.* 2009.

    2. *Fight for Freedom.* 2012.

Escape by Night: A Civil War Adventure. By Laurie Myers. Illustrated by Amy June Bates. Henry Holt, 2011.

Middle School

Crosswire. By Dotti Enderle. Calkins Creek, 2010.

Titanic (series). By Gordon Korman. Scholastic, 2011.

    1. *Unsinkable.*

    2. *Collision Course.*

    3. *S.O.S.*

Warriors in the Crossfire. By Nancy Bo Flood. Front Street, 2010.

Woods Runner. By Gary Paulsen. Wendy Lamb, 2010.

High School

The Berlin Boxing Club. By Robert Sharenow. HarperTeen, 2011.

The Coldest City. By Antony Johnston. Illustrated by Sam Hart. Oni Press, 2012.

Eleven Eleven. By Paul Dowswell. Bloomsbury, 2012.

Marathon. By Boaz Yakin and Joe Infurnari. First Second, 2012.

Shadow on the Mountain. By Margi Preus. Amulet, 2012.

Soldier Bear. By Bibi Dumon Tak. Translated by Laura Watkinson. Illustrated by Philip Hopman. Eerdmans, 2011.

Vietnam (series). By Chris Lynch. Scholastic.

    1. *I Pledge Allegiance.* 2011.

    2. *Sharpshooter.* 2012.

    3. *Free-Fire Zone.* 2012.

    4. *Casualties of War.* 2013.

History

Elementary

The Boston Tea Party. By Russell Freedman. Illustrated by Peter Malone. Holiday House, 2012.

Dogs on Duty: Soldiers' Best Friends on the Battlefield and Beyond. By Dorothy Hinshaw Patent. Walker, 2012.

For Liberty: The Story of the Boston Massacre; Addressed to the Inhabitants of America. By Timothy Decker. Calkins Creek, 2009.

An Inside Look at the U.S. Navy SEALs. By Joe Funk. Scholastic, 2011.

Middle School

Blizzard of Glass: The Halifax Explosion of 1917. By Sally M. Walker. Henry Holt, 2011.

Bomb: The Race to Build—and Steal—the World's Most Dangerous Weapon. By Steve Sheinkin. Roaring Brook, 2012.

Candy Bomber: The Story of the Berlin Airlift's "Chocolate Pilot." By Michael O. Tunnell. Charlesbridge, 2010.

Frederick Douglass for Kids: His Life and Times with 21 Activities. By Nancy I. Sanders. Chicago Review Press, 2012.

How They Croaked: The Awful Ends of the Awfully Famous. By Georgia Bragg. Illustrated by Kevin O'Malley. Walker, 2011.

Invincible Microbe: Tuberculosis and the Never-Ending Search for a Cure. By Jim Murphy and Alison Blank. Clarion, 2012.

Lincoln's Flying Spies: Thaddeus Lowe and the Civil War Balloon Corps. By Gail Jarrow. Calkins Creek, 2010.

Poop Happened! A History of the World from the Bottom Up. By Sarah Albee. Illustrated by Robert Leighton. Walker, 2010.

They Called Themselves the K.K.K.: The Birth of an American Terrorist Group. By Susan Campbell Bartoletti. Houghton Mifflin, 2010.

True Tales of the Wild West (series). By Jeff Savage. Enslow, 2012.

      1. American Cowboys

      2. Daring Pony Express Riders

      3. Fearless Scouts

      4. Pioneering Women

5. Quick-Draw Gunfighters

6. Rugged Gold Miners

High School

Beyond Courage: The Untold Story of Jewish Resistance during the Holocaust. By Doreen Rappaport. Candlewick, 2012.

Bloody Times: The Funeral of Abraham Lincoln and the Manhunt for Jefferson Davis. By James L. Swanson. Collins, 2011.

Chasing Lincoln's Killer. By James L. Swanson. Scholastic, 2009.

The Lost City of Z: A Tale of Deadly Obsession in the Amazon. By David Grann. Doubleday, 2009.

Signing Their Rights Away: The Fame and Misfortune of the Men Who Signed the United States Constitution. By Denise Kiernan and Joseph D'Agnese. Quirk Books, 2011.

The Smart Aleck's Guide to American History. By Adam Selzer. Delacorte, 2009.

Soldier Dogs: The Untold Story of America's Canine Heroes. By Maria Goodavage. Dutton, 2012.

Still I Rise: A Graphic History of African Americans. By Roland Laird with Taneshia Nash Laird. Illustrated by Elihu "Adofo" Bey. Sterling, 2009.

Taxes, the Tea Party, and Those Revolting Rebels: A History in Comics of the American Revolution. By Stan Mack. Nantier, Beall, Minoustchine, 2012.

Humor

Elementary

The Adventures of Ook and Gluk: Kung-Fu Cavemen from the Future. By Dav Pilkey. Blue Sky Press, 2010.

Dragonbreath (series) By Ursula Vernon. Dial.

    1. *Dragonbreath.* 2009.

    2. *Attack of the Ninja Frogs.* 2010.

    3. *Curse of the Were-Wiener.* 2010.

    4. *Lair of the Bat Monster.* 2011.

    5. *No Such Thing as Ghosts.* 2011.

    6. *Revenge of the Horned Bunnies.* 2012.

    7. *When Fairies Go Bad.* 2012.

    8. *Nightmare of the Iguana.* 2013.

    9. *The Case of the Toxic Mutants.* 2013.

The Flying Beaver Brothers (series). By Maxwell Eaton III. Knopf.

    1. *The Flying Beaver Brothers and the Evil Penguin Plan.* 2012.

    2. *The Flying Beaver Brothers and the Fishy Business.* 2012.

    3. *The Flying Beaver Brothers and the Mud-Slinging Moles.* 2013.

    4. *The Flying Beaver Brothers: Birds vs. Bunnies.* 2013.

Ghost Buddy (series). By Henry Winkler and Lin Oliver. Scholastic.

    1. *Zero to Hero.* 2012.

    2. *Mind If I Read Your Mind?* 2012.

    3. *How to Scare the Pants Off Your Pets.* 2013.

Jack and Jill Went Up to Kill: A Book of Zombie Nursery Rhymes. By Michael P. Spradlin. Illustrated by Jeff Weigel. Harper, 2011.

Just Joking: 300 Hilarious Jokes, Tricky Tongue Twisters, and Ridiculous Riddles. National Geographic, 2012.

Just Joking 2: 300 Hilarious Jokes about Everything, Including Tongue Twisters, Riddles, and More! National Geographic, 2012.

Lunch Lady (series). By Jarrett J. Krosoczka. Knopf.

    1. *Lunch Lady and the Cyborg Substitute.* 2009.

    2. *Lunch Lady and the League of Librarians.* 2009.

    3. *Lunch Lady and the Author Visit Vendetta.* 2009.

    4. *Lunch Lady and the Summer Camp Shakedown*. 2010.

    5. *Lunch Lady and the Bake Sale Bandit*. 2010.

    6. *Lunch Lady and the Field Trip Fiasco*. 2011.

    7. *Lunch Lady and the Mutant Mathletes*. 2012.

    8. *Lunch Lady and the Picture Day Peril*. 2012.

    9. *Lunch Lady and the Video Game Villain*. 2013.

Stone Rabbit (series). By Erik Craddock. Random House.

    1. *BC Mambo*. 2009.

    2. *Pirate Palooza*. 2009.

    3. *Deep-Space Disco*. 2009.

    4. *Superhero Stampede*. 2010.

    5. *Ninja Slice*. 2010.

    6. *Night of the Living Dust Bunnies*. 2011.

    7. *Dragon Boogie*. 2012.

    8. *Robot Frenzy*. 2013.

Middle School

Archvillain (series). By Barry Lyga. Scholastic.

    1. *Archvillain*. 2010.

    2. *The Mad Mask*. 2012.

    3. *Yesterday Again*. 2013.

Big Nate (series). By Lincoln Peirce. Harper.

    1. *Big Nate: In a Class by Himself.* 2010.

    2. *Big Nate Strikes Again*. 2010.

    3. *Big Nate on a Roll*. 2011.

    4. *Big Nate Goes for Broke*. 2012.

    5. *Big Nate: What Could Possibly Go Wrong?* 2012.

    6. *Big Nate: Here Goes Nothing*. 2012.

    7. *Big Nate Flips Out*. 2013.

Bro-Jitsu: The Martial Art of Sibling Smackdown. By Daniel H. Wilson. Illustrated by Les McClaine. Bloomsbury, 2010.

Chomp. By Carl Hiaasen. Knopf, 2012.

The Creature from the Seventh Grade: Boy or Beast? By Bob Balaban. Illustrated by Andy Rash. Viking, 2012.

Dead End in Norvelt. By Jack Gantos. Farrar, Straus and Giroux, 2011.

I Funny: A Middle School Story. By James Patterson and Chris Grabenstein. Illustrated by Laura Park. Little, Brown, 2012.

Mush! Sled Dogs with Issues. By Glenn Eichler and Joe Infurnari. First Second, 2011.

Planet Tad. By Tim Carvell. Illustrated by Doug Holgate. Harper, 2012.

Poop Happened! A History of the World from the Bottom Up. By Sarah Albee. Illustrated by Robert Leighton. Walker, 2010.

The Talent Show. By Dan Gutman. Simon and Schuster, 2010.

Ungifted. By Gordon Korman. Balzer and Bray, 2012.

High School

The Second Base Club. By Greg Trine. Henry Holt, 2010.

Sidekicks. By Jack D. Ferraiolo. Amulet, 2011.

Swim the Fly (series). By Don Calame. Candlewick.

    1. Swim the Fly. 2009.

    2. Beat the Band. 2010.

    3. Call the Shots. 2012.

Thou Shalt Not Road Trip. By Antony John. Dial, 2012.

Elementary

The Cartoon Chronicles of America (series). By Stan Mack and Susan Champlin. Bloomsbury.

    1. *Road to Revolution.* 2009.

    2. *Fight for Freedom.* 2012.

Dogs on Duty: Soldiers' Best Friends on the Battlefield and Beyond. By Dorothy Hinshaw Patent. Walker, 2012.

Escape by Night: A Civil War Adventure. By Laurie Myers. Illustrated by Amy June Bates. Henry Holt, 2011.

For Liberty: The Story of the Boston Massacre; Addressed to the Inhabitants of America. By Timothy Decker. Calkins Creek, 2009.

An Inside Look at the U.S. Navy SEALs. By Joe Funk. Scholastic, 2011.

Saving the Baghdad Zoo: A True Story of Hope and Heroes. By Kelly Milner Halls and William Sumner. Greenwillow, 2010.

Middle School

Bomb: The Race to Build—and Steal—the World's Most Dangerous Weapon. By Steve Sheinkin. Roaring Brook, 2012.

Candy Bomber: The Story of the Berlin Airlift's "Chocolate Pilot." By Michael O. Tunnell. Charlesbridge, 2010.

Lincoln's Flying Spies: Thaddeus Lowe and the Civil War Balloon Corps. By Gail Jarrow. Calkins Creek, 2010.

Warriors in the Crossfire. By Nancy Bo Flood. Front Street, 2010.

Woods Runner. By Gary Paulsen. Wendy Lamb, 2010.

High School

The Assault. By Brian Faulkner. Recon Team Angel series, book 1. Random House, 2012.

Bloody Times: The Funeral of Abraham Lincoln and the Manhunt for Jefferson Davis. By James L. Swanson. Collins, 2011.

Eleven Eleven. By Paul Dowswell. Bloomsbury, 2012.

The Leviathan Trilogy (series). By Scott Westerfeld. Illustrated by Keith Thompson. Simon Pulse.

    1. *Leviathan*. 2009.

    2. *Behemoth*. 2010.

    3. *Goliath*. 2011.

Marathon. By Boaz Yakin and Joe Infurnari. First Second, 2012.

Shadow on the Mountain. By Margi Preus. Amulet, 2012.

Soldier Bear. By Bibi Dumon Tak. Translated by Laura Watkinson. Illustrated by Philip Hopman. Eerdmans, 2011.

Soldier Dogs: The Untold Story of America's Canine Heroes. By Maria Goodavage. Dutton, 2012.

Taxes, the Tea Party, and Those Revolting Rebels: A History in Comics of the American Revolution. By Stan Mack. Nantier, Beall, Minoustchine, 2012.

Vietnam (series)

    1. *I Pledge Allegiance*. By Chris Lynch. Scholastic, 2011.

    2. *Sharpshooter*. By Chris Lynch. Scholastic, 2012.

    3. *Free-Fire Zone*. By Chris Lynch. Scholastic, 2012.

    4. *Casualties of War*. By Chris Lynch. Scholastic, 2013.

The Warrior's Heart: Becoming a Man of Compassion and Courage. By Eric Greitens. Houghton Mifflin, 2012.

Science

Elementary

Afraid of the Water (series). Bearport, 2010.

> 1. *Blue-Ringed Octopus: Small but Deadly*. By Natalie Lunis.
>
> 2. *Box Jellyfish: Killer Tentacles*. By Natalie Lunis.
>
> 3. *Moray Eel: Dangerous Teeth*. By Meish Goldish.
>
> 4. *Portuguese Man-of-War: Floating Misery*. By Natalie Lunis.
>
> 5. *Shark: The Shredder*. By Meish Goldish.
>
> 6. *Stonefish: Needles of Pain*. By Meish Goldish.

Baby Mammoth Mummy: Frozen in Time! A Prehistoric Animal's Journey into the 21st Century. By Christopher Sloan with Bernard Buigues. Photographs by Francis Latreille. National Geographic, 2011.

Barnum's Bones: How Barnum Brown Discovered the Most Famous Dinosaur in the World. By Tracy Fern. Illustrated by Boris Kulikov. Farrar, Straus and Giroux, 2012.

Big Cats: In Search of Lions, Leopards, Cheetahs, and Tigers. By Steve Bloom. Thames and Hudson, 2012.

Biggest, Baddest Book of Beasts. By Anders Hanson and Elissa Mann. ABDO, 2013.

The Case of the Vanishing Golden Frogs: A Scientific Mystery. By Sandra Markle. Millbrook Press, 2012.

Mysteries of the Komodo Dragon: The Biggest, Deadliest Lizard Gives Up Its Secrets. By Marty Crump. Boyds Mills Press, 2010.

Middle School

Adventure Beneath the Sea: Living in an Underwater Science Station. By Kenneth Mallory. Photographs by Brian Skerry. Boyds Mills Press, 2010.

Albert Einstein and Relativity for Kids: His Life and Ideas with 21 Activities and Thought Experiments. By Jerome Pohlen. Chicago Review Press, 2012.

Awesome Snake Science! 40 Activities for Learning about Snakes. By Cindy Blobaum. Chicago Review Press, 2012.

50 Poisonous Questions: A Book with Bite. By Tanya Lloyd Kyi. Illustrated by Ross Kinnaird. Annick Press, 2011.

Here There Be Monsters: The Legendary Kraken and the Giant Squid. By H. P. Newquist. Houghton Mifflin, 2010.

Invincible Microbe: Tuberculosis and the Never-Ending Search for a Cure. By Jim Murphy and Alison Blank. Clarion, 2012.

Nightmare Plagues (series). Bearport, 2011.

    1. *Bubonic Plague: The Black Death!* By Stephen Person.

    2. *The Flu of 1918: Millions Dead Worldwide!* By Jessica Rudolph.

    3. *Malaria: Super Killer!* By Stephen Person.

    4. *Smallpox: Is It Over?* By Adam Reingold.

    5. *Tuberculosis: The White Plague!* By Miriam Aronin.

    6. *Typhoid Fever: Dirty Food, Dirty Water!* By William Caper.

The Ultimate Survival Guide. By Mike Flynn. Illustrated by Mike Phillips. Macmillan, 2010.

High School

Bulu: African Wonder Dog. By Dick Houston. Random House, 2010.

Electrified Sheep: Glass-Eating Scientists, Nuking the Moon, and More Bizarre Experiments. By Alex Boese. Thomas Dunne Books, 2012.

The Lost City of Z: A Tale of Deadly Obsession in the Amazon. By David Grann. Doubleday, 2009.

Science Fiction

Elementary

Aliens on Vacation. By Clete Barrett Smith. Illustrated by Christian Slade. Disney/Hyperion, 2011.

Darth Vader and Son. By Jeffrey Brown. Chronicle Books, 2012.

Middle School

Archvillain (series). By Barry Lyga. Scholastic.

    1. *Archvillain.* 2010.

    2. *The Mad Mask.* 2012.

    3. *Yesterday Again.* 2013.

Bad Island. By Doug TenNapel. Graphix, 2011.

The Creature from the Seventh Grade: Boy or Beast? By Bob Balaban. Illustrated by Andy Rash. Viking, 2012.

Erebos. By Ursula Poznanski. Translated by Judith Pattinson. Annick Press, 2012.

Joshua Dread. By Lee Bacon. Delacorte, 2012.

High School

Amped. By Daniel H. Wilson. Doubleday, 2012.

The Assault. By Brian Faulkner. Recon Team Angel series, book 1. Random House, 2012.

Crater: A Helium-3 Novel. By Homer Hickam. Thomas Nelson, 2012.

Failstate. By John W. Otte. Marcher Lord, 2012.

Galactic Football League (series). By Scott Sigler. Diversion Books.

    1. *The Rookie.* 2009.

    2. *The Starter.* 2010.

    3. *The All-Pro.* 2011.

    4. *The MVP.* 2012.

The Griff. By Christopher Moore and Ian Corson with Jennyson Rosero. William Morrow, 2011.

The Klaatu Diskos (series). By Pete Hautman. Candlewick.

    1. *The Obsidian Blade*. 2012.

    2. *The Cydonian Pyramid*. 2013.

The Leviathan Trilogy (series). By Scott Westerfeld. Illustrated by Keith Thompson. Simon Pulse.

    1. *Leviathan*. 2009.

    2. *Behemoth*. 2010.

    3. *Goliath*. 2011.

Michael Vey (series). By Richard Paul Evans. Simon Pulse.

    1. *Michael Vey: The Prisoner of Cell 25*. 2011.

    2. *Michael Vey: Rise of the Elgen*. 2012.

Monument 14. By Emmy Laybourne. Feiwel and Friends, 2012.

The Paladin Prophecy. By Mark Frost. Random House, 2012.

Ready Player One. By Ernest Cline. Crown, 2011.

Replication: The Jason Experiment. By Jill Williamson. Zondervan, 2011.

Robopocalypse. By Daniel H. Wilson. Doubleday, 2011.

Sidekicks. By Jack D. Ferraiolo. Amulet, 2011.

The Unwind Trilogy (series). By Neal Shusterman. Simon and Schuster.

    1. *Unwind*. 2009.

    2. *UnWholly*. 2012.

    3. *UnSouled*. 2013.

Sports

Elementary

Brothers at Bat: The True Story of an Amazing All-Brother Baseball Team. By Audrey Vernick. Illustrated by Steven Salerno. Clarion, 2012. (Baseball)

Fred Bowen Sports Stories (series). By Fred Bowen. Peachtree.

1. *Soccer Team Upset.* 2009. (Soccer)
2. *Touchdown Trouble.* 2009. (Football)
3. *Dugout Rivals.* 2010. (Baseball)
4. *Hardcourt Comeback.* 2010. (Basketball)
5. *Throwing Heat.* 2010. (Baseball)
6. *Quarterback Season.* 2011. (Football)
7. *Real Hoops.* 2011. (Basketball)
8. *Go for the Goal!* 2012. (Soccer)
9. *Perfect Game.* 2013. (Baseball)

Game-Day Youth (series). By Suzy Beamer Bohnert. B&B Publishing.

1. *Game-Day Youth: Learning Baseball's Lingo.* 2010. (Baseball)
2. *Game-Day Youth: Learning Basketball's Lingo.* 2011. (Basketball)

No Easy Way: The Story of Ted Williams and the Last .400 Season. By Fred Bowen. Illustrated by Charles S. Pyle. Dutton, 2010. (Baseball)

Topps League Stories (series) (Baseball). By Kurtis Scaletta. Amulet.

1. *Jinxed!* Illustrated by Eric Wight. 2012.
2. *Steal That Base!* Illustrated by Eric Wight. 2012.
3. *Zip It!* Illustrated by Eric Wight. 2012.
4. *The 823rd Hit.* Illustrated by Eric Wight. 2012.
5. *You're Out!* Illustrated by Ethen Beavers. 2013.
6. *Batter Up!* Illustrated by Ethen Beavers. 2013.

X-Moves (series) (Extreme Sports). By Michael Sandler. Bearport, 2010.

1. *Cool Snowboarders*
2. *Daring BMXers*
3. *Gnarly Skateboarders*
4. *Mighty MotoXers*
5. *Rally Car Dudes*
6. *Super Surfers*

Middle School

Cal Ripken Jr.'s All-Stars (series) (Baseball). By Cal Ripken Jr. with Kevin Cowherd. Disney/Hyperion.

> 1. *Hothead.* 2011.
>
> 2. *Super-Sized Slugger.* 2012.
>
> 3. *Wild Pitch.* 2013.

Game Changers (series). By Mike Lupica. Scholastic.

> 1. *Game Changers.* 2012. (Football)
>
> 2. *Play Makers.* 2013. (Basketball)

Hammerin' Hank Greenberg: Baseball Pioneer. By Shelley Sommer. Calkins Creek, 2011. (Baseball)

Lucky: Maris, Mantle, and My Best Summer Ever. By Wes Tooke. Simon and Schuster, 2010. (Baseball)

Pinch Hit. By Tim Green. Harper, 2012. (Baseball)

Playing for Keeps. By Steven Sandor. Lorimer, 2012. (Soccer)

The Underdogs. By Mike Lupica. Philomel, 2011. (Football)

Unstoppable. By Tim Green with Barbara Lalicki. Harper, 2012. (Football)

High School

The Berlin Boxing Club. By Robert Sharenow. HarperTeen, 2011. (Boxing)

Boy21. By Matthew Quick. Little, Brown, 2012. (Basketball)

Calico Joe. By John Grisham. Doubleday, 2012. (Baseball)

Galactic Football League (series) (Football). By Scott Sigler. Diversion Books.

> 1. *The Rookie.* 2009.
>
> 2. *The Starter.* 2010.
>
> 3. *The All-Pro.* 2011.
>
> 4. *The MVP.* 2012.

Gil Marsh. By A. C. E. Bauer. Random House, 2012. (Cross Country Running)

Last Ride. By Laura Langston. Orca, 2011. (Auto Racing)

No Dribbling the Squid: Octopush, Shin Kicking, Elephant Polo, and Other Oddball Sports. By Michael J. Rosen with Ben Kassoy. Andrews McMeel, 2009. (Unusual Sports)

Payback Time. By Carl Deuker. Houghton Mifflin, 2010. (Football)

Pick-Up Game: A Full Day of Full Court. Edited by Marc Aronson and Charles R. Smith Jr. Candlewick, 2011. (Basketball)

True Legend. By Mike Lupica. Philomel, 2012. (Basketball)

Bibliography

"The Almost Completely True Adventures of Dav Pilkey." www.pilkey.com, accessed August 28, 2012.

Austin, Liz. "More U.S. Schools Segregating Sexes." *Associated Press*, August 24, 2004.

Below, Jamie L., et al. "Gender Differences in Early Literacy: Analysis of Kindergarten through Fifth-Grade Dynamic Indicators of Basic Early Literacy Skills Probes." *School Psychology Review*, 2010, 240–57.

Bickford, Jill. "Consumerism: How It Impacts Play and Its Presence in Library Collections." *Children and Libraries*, Winter 2010, 53–56.

Bloom, Adi. "Girls Go for Little Women but Boys Prefer Lara." *Times Educational Supplement*, March 15, 2002, 18.

Brizendine, Louann. *The Male Brain*. Broadway Books, 2010.

Brozo, William G. "Bridges to Literacy for Boys." *Educational Leadership*, September 2006, 71–74.

——. "Gender and Reading Literacy." *Reading Today*, February/March 2005, 18.

——. *To Be a Boy, To Be a Reader*. International Reading Association, 2002.

Carlsson-Paige, Nancy, and Diane E. Levin. *Who's Calling the Shots? How to Respond Effectively to Children's Fascination with War Play, War Toys and Violent TV*. New Society Publishers, 1990.

Cavazos-Kottke, Sean. "Five Readers Browsing: The Reading Interests of Talented Middle School Boys." *Gifted Child Quarterly*, Spring 2006, 132–47.

Clark, Christina, and Kate Rumbold. "Reading for Pleasure: A Research Overview." *National Literacy Trust*, November 2006.

Clavel, Matthew. "Save the Males: A Case for Making Schools Friendlier to Boys." *American Enterprise*, July/August 2005, 30–32.

Dillon, Karen. "No Girls Allowed: Men Bond over Books." *Roanoke Times*, August 3, 2007, C1.

Doiron, Roy. "Boy Books, Girl Books." *Teacher Librarian*, February 2003, 14–16.

Duncan, Melanie C. "A Born-Again Genre." *Library Journal*, February 15, 2012, 26.

"Educators Keep an Eye on Boys-Only Experiment at Thornton Academy." *Associated Press*, February 10, 2008.

Elias, Marilyn. "Electronic World Swallows Up Kids' Time, Study Finds." *USA Today*, March 10, 2005, A1.

Fairbanks North Star Borough Public Library. *Guys Read Pilot Program: Final Report* (2007).

Farris, Pamela J., et al. "Male Call: Fifth-Grade Boys' Reading Preferences." *Reading Teacher*, November 2009, 180–88.

Fine, Jon. "Where the Boys Aren't." *Businessweek*, November 7, 2005, 24.

Fine, Sean. "Schools Told to Fix Boys' Low Grades." *Globe and Mail*, August 27, 2001, http://v1.theglobeandmail.com/series/school/fix.html.

Flannery, Mary Ellen. "No Girls Allowed." *NEA Today*, April 2006, www.nea.org/home/12376.htm.

Fletcher, Ralph. *Boy Writers: Reclaiming Their Voices*. Stenhouse, 2006.

Follos, Alison M. G. *Reviving Reading: School Library Programming, Author Visits and Books That Rock!* Libraries Unlimited, 2006.

Fulghum, Robert. *It Was on Fire When I Lay Down on It*. Villard, 1989.

Gandolfo, Anita. *Faith and Fiction: Christian Literature in America Today*. Praeger, 2007.

Gottschall, Jonathan. *The Storytelling Animal: How Stories Make Us Human*. Houghton Mifflin, 2012.

Greene, J., and M. Winters. *Leaving Boys Behind: Public High School Graduation Rates*. Manhattan Institute, 2006. www.manhattan-institute.org/html/cr_48.htm.

Gurian, Michael, and Patricia Henley, with Terry Trueman. *Boys and Girls Learn Differently! A Guide for Teachers and Parents*. Jossey-Bass, 2001.

Hannaford, Carla. *Smart Moves: Why Learning Is Not All in Your Head*. Great Ocean Publishers, 1995.

Hole, Carol. "Click! The Feminization of the Public Library: Policies and Attitudes Make Men the Great Unserved." *American Libraries*, December 1990, 1076–79.

Howe, James. *Screaming Mummies of the Pharaoh's Tomb II*. Atheneum Books for Young Readers, 2003.

Ingles, Steven J., et al. *A Profile of the American Sophomore in 2002: Initial Results from the Base Year of the Education Longitudinal Study of 2002*. National Center for Education Statistics, 2005.

Jones, Patrick, and Dawn Cartwright Fiorelli. "Overcoming the Obstacle Course: Teenage Boys and Reading." *Teacher Librarian*, February 2003, 9–13.

Keddie, Amanda. "Feminist Struggles to Mobilise Progressive Spaces within the 'Boy-Turn' in Gender Equity and Schooling Reform." *Gender and Education*, July 2010, 353–68.

Kimura, Doreen. "Sex Differences in the Brain." *Scientific American*, September 1992, 26–31.

Kipnis, Aaron. *Angry Young Men: How Parents, Teachers, and Counselors Can Help "Bad Boys" Become Good Men*. Jossey-Bass, 2002.

Krashen, Stephen D. *The Power of Reading: Insights from the Research*. 2nd ed. Libraries Unlimited, 2004.

Lesesne, Teri S. *Naked Reading: Uncovering What Tweens Need to Become Lifelong Readers*. Stenhouse, 2006.

Lingo, Sandra. "The All Guys Book Club: Where Boys Take the Risk to Read." *Library Media Connection*, April/May 2007, 24–28.

Miller, Donalyn. *The Book Whisperer*. Jossey-Bass, 2009.

Miranda, Twyla, et al. "Reluctant Readers in Middle School: Successful Engagement with Text Using the E-reader." *International Journal of Applied Science and Technology*, November 2011, 81–91.

Morley, Judith A., and Sandra E. Russell. "Making Literature Meaningful: A Classroom/Library Partnership." In *Battling Dragons: Issues and Controversy in Children's Literature*. Heinemann, 1995.

Moyer, Mary, and Melissa Williams. "Personal Programming." *Knowledge Quest*, March/April 2011, 68–73.

Pennac, Daniel. *Better Than Life*. Coach House Press, 1994.

Pirie, B. *Teenage Boys and High School English*. Heinemann, 2002.

Pomerantz, Eva M., Ellen Rydell Altermatt, and Jill L. Saxon. "Making the Grade but Feeling Distressed: Gender Differences in Academic Performance and Internal Distress." *Journal of Educational Psychology*, June 2002, 396–404.

Pottorff, Donald D., Deborah Phelps-Zientarski, and Michelle E. Skovera. "Gender Perceptions of Elementary and Middle School Students about Literacy at Home and School." *Journal of Research and Development in Education*, Summer 1996, 203–11.

Rainie, Lee, et al. *The Rise of E-reading*. Pew Research Center's Internet and American Life Project, 2012.

Rideout, Victoria J., Elizabeth A. Vandewater, and Ellen A. Wartella. *Zero to Six: Electronic Media in the Lives of Infants, Toddlers and Preschoolers*. Henry J. Kaiser Family Foundation, 2003.

Riess, Jana. "Christian YA Fiction Still Finding Its Footing." *Publishers Weekly*, August 15, 2011, 30–31.

Ripley, Amanda. "Who Says a Woman Can't Be Einstein?" *Time*, March 7, 2005, 55.

Robinson, Christine. "A Developmental Difference." *Casper Star Tribune*, August 1, 2007, http://trib.com/news/article_d80a9c9d-e083-53f9-8811-6a3037ac5bb1.html.

Ross, Catherine Sheldrick, Lynne (E. F.) McKechnie, and Paulette M. Rothbauer. *Reading Matters: What the Research Reveals about Reading, Libraries, and Community*. Libraries Unlimited, 2006.

Royer, James M., and Rachel E. Wing. "Making Sense of Sex Differences in Reading and Math Assessment: The Practice and Engagement Hypothesis." *Issues in Education*, 2002, 77–86.

Sanford, Kathy, Heather Blair, and Raymond Chodzinski. "A Conversation about Boys and Literacy." *Teaching and Learning*, Spring 2007, 4–14.

Sax, Leonard. "The Boy Problem." *School Library Journal*, September 2007, 40–43.

——. *Boys Adrift: The Five Factors Driving the Growing Epidemic of Unmotivated Boys and Underachieving Young Men*. Basic Books, 2007.

——. *Why Gender Matters: What Parents and Teachers Need to Know about the Emerging Science of Sex Differences*. Doubleday, 2005.

Schneider, Helen. "My Child and ADHD: Chances of Being Diagnosed." *Pediatrics for Parents*, September 2007, 9–11.

"School Experiments with Same-Sex Reading Groups." *Curriculum Review*, April 2005, 8.

Scieszka, Jon. "Guys and Reading." *Teacher Librarian*, February 2003, 17–18.

Sommers, Christina Hoff. *The War against Boys*. Simon and Schuster, 2000.

Steiner, Stan. "Where Have All the Men Gone? Male Role Models in the Reading Crisis." *PNLA Quarterly*, Summer 2000, 17.

Strauss, Valerie. "Educators Differ on Why Boys Lag in Reading." *Washington Post*, March 15, 2005, A12.

Taliaferro, Lanning. "Education Gender Gap Leaving Boys Behind." *Journal News*, June 17, 2001, 17.

Taylor, Donna Lester. "'Not Just Boring Stories': Reconsidering the Gender Gap for Boys." *Journal of Adolescent and Adult Literacy*, December 2004/January 2005, 290–98.

Toppo, Greg. "Funny, but Boys Do Read." *USA Today*, July 6, 2005, Life, 8D.

Tunnell, Michael O., and James S. Jacobs. "Series Fiction and Young Readers." *Booklist*, September 15, 2005, 64–65.

Tyre, Peg. *The Trouble with Boys: A Surprising Report Card on Our Sons, Their Problems at School, and What Parents and Educators Must Do*. Crown Publishers, 2008.

Ujiie, Joanne, and Stephen Krashen. "Are Prize-Winning Books Popular among Children? An Analysis of Public Library Circulation." *Knowledge Quest*, January/February 2006, 33–35.

Whitmire, Richard. "Boy Trouble." *New Republic*, January 23, 2006, 15–18.

——. *Why Boys Fail: Saving Our Sons from an Educational System That's Leaving Them Behind*. American Management Association, 2010.

Wilhelm, Jeffrey D., and Michael Smith. "Asking the Right Questions: Literate Lives of Boys." *Reading Teacher*, May 2005, 788–89.

——. *Reading Don't Fix No Chevys: Literacy in the Lives of Young Men*. Heinemann, 2002.

Winerip, Michael. "In a Standardized Era, a Creative School Is Forced to Be More So." *New York Times*, October 30, 2011, www.nytimes.com/2011/10/31 /education/no-child-left-behind-catches-up-with-new-hampshire-school .html.

Young, Josephine Peyton, and William G. Brozo. "Boys Will Be Boys, or Will They? Literacy and Masculinities." *Reading Research Quarterly*, July/August/ September 2001, 316–25.

Index